THAT'S MEN

The best of the 'That's Men' column from *The Irish Times*

D0893061

Padraig O'Morain

VERITAS

First published 2008 by
Veritas Publications
7/8 Lower Abbey Street
Dublin 1
Ireland
Email publications@veritas.ie
Website www.veritas.ie

ISBN 978 1 84730 101 7

A catalogue record for this book is available from the British Library.

Cover design Paula Ryan
Printed in the Republic of Ireland by Betaprint Ltd., Dublin

Veritas books are printed on paper made from the wood pulp of managed forests. For every tree felled, at least one tree is planted, thereby renewing natural resources.

To Phil, Niamh and Hannah

Acknowledgements

Barry O'Keeffe, editor of the *Irish Times* health supplement, HEALTHplus, has nurtured the men's column throughout most of its existence.

Kevin O'Sullivan originally commissioned the column.

Those custodians of the soul of a newspaper, the sub-editors, have cast a benevolent eye on my efforts.

My thanks to all.

Contents

Introduction

That's Men aims to fill a gap. Newspapers and magazines have devoted millions of words and pictures to women's physical, mental and emotional health, to how they look, to what they wear and to their relationships.

This interest is not all benevolent, of course. It is partly driven by that huge industry which exists to sell products and services to women for their minds, bodies and emotions.

In all of this, though, men's health and relationships have been largely ignored. Indeed, the concept of men's health is often confined to the physical – prostate cancer, for instance – as if we don't have a psychology or as if our psychology is too crude to bother about.

In commissioning this column for the *Irish Times* health supplement HEALTHplus, Kevin O'Sullivan, and his successor Barry O'Keeffe, sought to change this imbalance.

Sex, depression, fun, bullying, relationship enhancement, fatherhood and many other topics have since featured in 'That's Men' (originally titled 'That's Men for You'). Men have welcomed the column but so have women, especially when it deals with relationships. Some columns, particularly those which address fatherhood, have led to lively discussions on my *Just Like A Man* blog (www.justlikeaman.blogspot.com).

The column mirrors the diversity and sometimes contrariness of life. Coping with Christmas, living with post-natal depression, the joys of sleeping in separate bedrooms, whether men are more likely than women to be sent to the doghouse, accepting conflict in relationships and the very real difficulties in communication between the genders have all been aired.

Along the way, the column has informed, amused, entertained and sometimes irritated and enraged readers. Long may it continue to do so.

Padraig O'Morain

We need to talk

What are the four scariest words a woman can utter to a man? Forget candidates such as 'Will you marry me?' or 'I'm having your baby'. No, the scariest words are, 'We need to talk'.

The woman may think it's a great idea to have a talk about some difficult issue in the relationship, get it all out in the open, talk it through etc. However, as soon as the man hears these words his blood pressure rises, alarm bells start clamouring in his mind and he assumes a hunted, haunted look.

It's like driving down the road and noticing there's a Garda motorcycle behind you: even if you have been keeping within the speed limit, that part of your mind that is forever a schoolboy immediately assumes you have done something wrong.

Fortunately, the motorcycle cop usually continues on about his business. The woman who has declared that 'We need to talk', however, does not.

By the time the 'talk' comes around, the man is well and truly in his cave, hiding in the deep shadows. He may even fling the occasional rock – in the form of a defensive comment – towards the entrance to repel intruders.

Because most women will talk about their feelings at the drop of a hat, they do not necessarily realise that their partner is in a state of paranoia. I have noticed in my work as a counsellor – the woman in my life is, of course, perfect – that women are very, very good at expressing themselves. As a matter of fact, they are too good at it.

The woman expresses her feelings comprehensively and with great precision. The occasional little barb may be launched. John 'chooses' to play 'his' golf on a Saturday morning instead of spending the time with 'his' kids. In vain does John protest that the kids would rather be playing with their Playstations or watching Nickelodeon than bonding with Dad. Perhaps they might spend less time watching television if they had a father who showed an interest in them, he is told. John retreats back into his cave, growling and grinding his teeth.

The thing is, for all their gift at talking about their feelings, women can come across badly. They often fail to understand that the man does not see himself as engaging in a conversation between equals. The man – if we may leave the cave for a moment – sees himself as the prisoner standing in the dock while a lengthy charge sheet is read out. Instead of engaging with the woman, he pleads 'not guilty' and waits to be taken down to the cells.

This is why men can come across so badly too. The man defends himself, stonewalls or attacks back. The more frustrated the woman gets with this the more she presses forward and the more he retreats. In the end, everybody is angry, frustrated and fed up.

What's to be done? Here are four thoughts that might help men in communicating with women about difficult issues:

1. Generally speaking, women prefer to talk about problems than not to talk about them. There is nothing to gain from pretending to be a superman with no problems. As a matter of fact, if you don't have any problems, perhaps you should make one up just so you can both have a nice chat about it.

2. Women like to express feelings and it wouldn't kill you to express your feelings occasionally too. Here's a trick: instead of telling her what happened at work today, tell her how you felt at work today.

3. The next time your partner wants to talk, look her in the eye and see if there is anything in what she says that you agree with. Then agree with it. See what happens.

4. If you want to take a rise out of her, stroll up when she's least expecting it and say, 'We need to talk'!

And what have I to say to the women? Er, nothing. This column is for men. Go away. I deny everything. I am innocent. I have to leave now.

All the money but none of the fun

'I have a rich neighbour who is always so busy that he has no leisure to laugh; the whole business of his life is to get money, more money, so that he may get still more. He considers not that it is not in the power of riches to make a man happy; for it was wisely said that there be as many miseries beyond riches as on this side of them.'

I was reminded of that quote from Izaak Walton, author of *The Compleat Angler*, by a piece of research that has recently been published in *Science* magazine. It concerns money and happiness, and it makes me wonder if we are all mad. As you know, for the past number of years we have been living in a booming little country and many of us are frantically trying to make money to pay the bills – or just trying to make money. Behind all this activity is the assumption that our lives will, somehow, be better if we have more money.

However, the report in *Science* confirms what Walton knew back in the seventeenth century: an increase in income does not bring significant increases in happiness. According to the article, US government statistics show that men who make more than $100,000 a year spend about 20 per cent of their time in leisure activities. Men who make less than $20,000 a year get to spend about 35 per cent of their time on leisure activities. The figures for women are similar.

Previous research, done back in the 1990s, shows that leisure is, perhaps, the main source of happiness. Among the leisure activities, the ones that seem to bring greatest satisfaction are those that involve activities, meeting challenges and so on. 'Passive leisure' seems to bring happiness as well. For example, soap operas provide us with imaginary people to whom we can relate. Leisure activities often involve the company of friends, which also seems to make us happier. Even hours spent on bebo.com and myspace.com (teens and tweens consider it obligatory to be on both at the same time) involve interaction with people.

If people on higher incomes spend much less time in leisure than people on lower incomes, then an important source of happiness is closed off to them. Bureau of Labour statistics in the US show that people with higher incomes spend more of their time in 'obligatory' activities such as working, shopping and childcare. The researchers found that these activities were linked with higher tension and stress. I bet a lot of people in this country can relate to that in a big way.

In their book, *The Psychology of Money*, Adrian Furnham and Michael Argyle point out that 'lack of money can limit leisure, but much leisure is free or nearly so – church, evening classes, walking, the public library and voluntary work'. Yet there are many, many people for whom these sources of leisure are unattainable. They just do not have the time for them. We are money rich and time poor.

Why doesn't more money make us happier? One key reason, according to Furnham and Argyle, is that once we have that extra money we just get used to it. Before we get our hands on the money we tell ourselves how wonderful it would be to have all that extra dosh. But once we've got it, well, we've got it and the buzz disappears. What's more, we have a habit of comparing ourselves with people who have more money – and no matter how much we have there will always be someone who has more.

What makes us humans so maddening is that I know all this stuff but I'm going to keep on buying Lotto tickets. And I'm still going to try to earn more money this year than I earned last year. Illogical and irrational? Absolutely, no question about it.

Will I ever give up the illusory pursuit of happiness through income and enjoy the simple life instead? Of course. Just as soon as I can afford it.

Mirror, mirror on the wall

Why is it that when you snap at your significant other, she snaps back? And why is it that when she whispers sweet nothings in your ear, you purr like a marmalade cat?

Part of the answer to these questions – and some hints as to how we might improve our relationships – can be found in the existence of 'mirror neurons' in our brains. Put simply, mirror neurons ensure that if I see you being angry, my brain will 'mirror' your anger; if I see you being pleasant and comforting, than those parts of my brain that create the feeling of pleasantness and comfort will be activated.

You can study this phenomenon with MRI scans or by attaching electrodes to neurons in your brain, though it is not generally recommended to do this at home. Mirror neurons have been studied quite intensively for more than ten years now and I suspect that they are about to become the next big thing. I suspect this because Daniel Goleman, whose book *Emotional Intelligence* was one of the big things of the last ten years, made mirror neurons the subject of his most recent book, *Social Intelligence*.

Each thought, emotion or action we perform requires certain neurons (nerve cells) to activate. Researchers at the University of Parma in Italy discovered ten years ago that if you watch somebody performing an activity, the same nerve cells will activate in your brain as in theirs. Further work in Italy, France and the US even suggests that when you watch or hear a person expressing an emotion, the network of neurons that corresponds to that emotion activates in your own brain.

Have you ever noticed that there are people who can 'bring you down' with their moaning and groaning? This is, at least partly, because as you observe their gloom, your 'gloom' neurons activate and the other person's gloom becomes part of your own experience. There are also people in your life – I hope – whose good humour takes you 'out of yourself' and you feel better when you are with them. As you observe their good humour, your 'good humour' neurons activate and you thereby get into a good mood.

How does it help to know this? I would suggest that this information is extremely valuable in helping us to improve relationships. If your partner is being a bit tetchy, you can realise that your brain is about to begin mirroring her tetchiness. You can then make a choice to stay calm or to follow her into a row. If you remain calm, good-humoured or sympathetic long enough for her brain to mirror your good humour, then there is a better chance that she will get out of her bad mood.

In short, if you want to get her into a good mood, your best chance of succeeding is to be in a good mood yourself and to persist in that good mood. Don't push this thing too far, though. If her tetchiness is due to you landing home from the office Christmas party at six in the morning with lipstick on your collar, then mirror neurons might not save you. There are limits.

Still, this information explains, I think, the value of emotional support. Giving emotional support to someone else actually changes what is going on in that other person's brain. This might explain why criticism annoys people so much. While you are expressing your criticism, the other person's brain is mirroring your anger. Therefore there is little chance of your criticism being welcomed by your listener.

Mirror neurons may even help explain why the bully in the workplace can have such a devastating effect on their victim. The contempt being expressed by the bully is actually mirrored in the victim's brain and becomes part of the victim's experience. The victim needs to learn to interrupt the mirroring by deliberately thinking different thoughts while the bully is speaking.

The basic lesson from this information is that you are more influential than you think you are: you get back what you give out.

Where is the girl in the mini-skirt now?

I don't know what boys in school are told about girls today, but back in the 1960s, the official version could be somewhat daunting.

I have never forgotten the religious doctrine class in which the Brother Superior informed us that if a boy had sex with a girl, he would have committed two sins. First, he would have endangered his own immortal soul; second, he would have destroyed a temple of the Holy Ghost.

I should add that a phrase such as 'had sex with' would have been considered far too extreme for the classroom at the time – the phrase used was probably something like 'committed a mortal sin with'. This, after all, was the era when the lines '... O, most wicked speed, to post/With such dexterity to incestuous sheets!' were censored out of our edition of *Hamlet*. We only knew about them because our English teacher had an uncensored edition and read them out.

As for the temple of the Holy Ghost, we were Catholic lads so we had a Da Vinci Code-like ability to decipher religious references. Therefore it was understood by all of us that the temples of the Holy Ghost were, well, girls. We had never thought of girls that way before and I wish the Brother Superior hadn't come up with that particular way of looking at them. It puts you off, it does, until you manage to consign it to the mental scrapheap.

That said, the view of women imparted to us in Naas CBS was probably more favourable than what is normally regarded as the traditional Church view. That view was put to us when we were sent up to a Jesuit retreat house. There, we spent three days in silence, an experience enlivened by an apoplectic description of a girl in a mini-skirt by one of the priests.

I think he was a man who took life too seriously. When he entered the room to lecture us, we stood politely, just like we had been taught by the Christian Brothers. He stopped and stared at us: 'When I come into the room, boys, you do not stand,' he intoned, 'you kneel.'

He followed that one by recounting his experience of taking a city bus and finding himself sitting opposite a girl in a mini-skirt. Did she have no regard for the temptation she was putting before young Catholic boys? His voice rose as he asked this. If she had no regard for the immortal souls of the boys to whom she was an occasion of sin, did she not have some regard at least for her own immortal soul? 'What of the Virgin?' he cried. What indeed, we asked ourselves, as we mentally contemplated the image of the girl in the mini-skirt. This girl, he declared, his face now red with rage, may as well have slapped the Virgin in the face as dress in this immoral way. Having thus thoroughly unsettled us, he then led us in prayer.

These incidents illustrate the dilemma growing boys and, I suppose, girls found themselves in at the time. We were caught between two worlds: in one world, a girl was a temple of the Holy Ghost; in the other, she was a mini-skirted occasion of sin. Sometimes the worlds collided: the mini-skirted girl who got pregnant outside marriage could find herself on her knees scrubbing a convent floor for two years, waiting for her baby to be adopted by Americans. If the father wanted to contact her, no such contact was allowed: letters were read on the way in and the way out and there was no possibility of surreptitious phone calls.

Here we are in the twenty-first century and most of us have, by now, shaken off the idea of the female as either the austere temple of the Holy Ghost or the dangerous temptress, destroyer of men's souls. I suppose the priest is pushing up the daisies. And the girl in the mini-skirt is, perhaps, a respectable reader of *The Irish Times* who occasionally shakes her head at the carry-on of young wans nowadays.

If you are contemplating suicide

If you are thinking of taking your own life, read this.

If taking your own life is on your mind, you are probably a young man in your late teens or early twenties. Of course, you may be an older man or a woman, but young men form the biggest risk group for suicide.

Whichever group you belong to, you are probably depressed to a greater or lesser extent. You find it difficult to see the positive things in your life. It is as if a veil has been drawn over them and you are allowed to see only the things that bring you pain.

These things may have something to do with other people: a broken relationship, conflict with someone you love or bullying, for instance. It is more likely, however, that they have something to do with you. You are looking at all the things that are wrong with you. Other people see the things that are right with you but you think they are mistaken, foolish or deceived.

I have met people who thought and felt like you and who wanted to take their lives but decided against it. Why? In almost every case it was the thought of the pain that their death would bring to other people.

I know your depression has told you that other people would be better off without you. You are wrong about this.

I have also met the relatives of people who have killed themselves and I can tell you that they are most certainly not better off without the person who died. What has happened is that the person who has died has taken all their pain and passed it on to those who remain behind.

The sad thing is that the pain felt by the person who died

would have ended sooner or later had they stayed alive and they would have lived reasonably satisfying lives. You probably don't believe this but I have met enough people who have turned away from suicide to know that it's true.

The person who takes their own life takes a temporary pain and passes it on as a lifelong hurt to those who remain behind. Some of the bereaved may turn to drink or drugs for comfort; they may become depressed or may eventually take their own lives. Most of the bereaved live with the pain, but do not doubt for a second that there is pain.

I am telling you this because I believe that suicidal people care more about other people than they do about themselves.

But what about you? Does choosing life mean choosing permanent pain? I don't believe that's what it means at all. What you are going through right now is not your whole life. It is only a part of it. If you can pull yourself through this and stay alive, I am 100 per cent certain that you can experience the same degree of contentment and happiness as other people experience. I have seen it happen many times.

What can you do? If you are suicidal you are probably paying more attention to your own inadequacies or sorrows than you are to what is going on around you. But brooding locks in the pain – so first, try to tear your attention away from painful feelings and thoughts and turn it to whatever is happening outside you. Talk to other people, be aware of sights and sounds, read a book, listen to music, go for a walk and notice your surroundings.

Second, connect with people. If you can, tell someone you trust about how you really feel. This could be a work colleague, a friend or relative. If they dismiss it, don't turn away in despair – they may just be scared of what you are saying. You could also talk to your GP or a counsellor. You could contact the Samaritans (1850 60 90 90) or a self-help group like GROW (1890 474 474), Aware (01–661 7211) or Recovery (01–626 0775).

Third, resolve not to pass your pain on to others by taking your own life. You cannot see it now but I promise a day will come when you will be very, very glad you spared other people the terrible pain of your suicide.

Post-natal depression affects men too

Post-natal depression is a condition that we tend to think of as affecting only the mothers of new-born babies, but fathers can be affected too.

About 10 per cent of women suffer post-natal depression. Estimates of the number of men who experience this condition range from about 4 per cent to about 10 per cent. Many of the causes of post-natal depression in men may be the same as in women. The arrival of a baby, especially of the first baby, turns people's worlds upside down, as any parent will tell you at the drop of a hat.

How can you possibly be up to the task of rearing this creature that has just appeared in your life? What will you do if it breaks when you pick it up? Moreover, you now have a family to support. The question of supporting the new family weighs heavily on some men's minds especially if the mother is taking time off paid work.

Then there are societal pressures. There is still an assumption out there that women are complete experts on babies from the moment they themselves are born and that men are clumsy, awkward and inept. This may leave both parents scared out of their wits. The woman may be terrified that she will be unable to live up to the expectation that she be the perfect mother and the man may fear that he will not measure up as even a good parent.

Something else has changed too. When the man and the woman got together, through marriage or some other commitment, the two, as the saying goes, became one. When baby comes along, the one becomes three. The man may experience, imagine or fear a great change in his relationship with his wife. After all, there is somebody else there now who is getting all the attention. This new arrival is apt to be more immediately demanding than either of the two people who were there first.

Therefore it's hardly surprising that the birth of a baby can bring on post-natal depression in either the mother or the father. Add to this the fact that the birth of a baby sometimes awakens for the woman the full impact of a previous emotional trauma. This, for instance, could be grief over the death of a parent or over a miscarriage that they did not deal with fully at the time. That grief can now hit her with full force, for reasons that we do not fully understand.

Does the same thing happen with fathers? We don't really know. If you think you may suffer from post-natal depression and you're a man – the same goes for women – it is very, very important that you go to your GP or a counsellor. Post-natal depression comes at a bad time: just when you need your strength to cope with a new and challenging situation, your strength disappears.

Everyone tells you what a wonderful baby you have and you don't know what they are talking about. You are afraid you are losing your mind. Your partner may be trying to help you, as well as coping with the baby, but you neither notice it nor appreciate it. You are drained of energy and everything that you used to do quickly and easily takes a long time to get through.

The demands of looking after a baby while you are depressed are very painful and you really shouldn't try to handle it on your own. There is some evidence that post-natal depression, if untreated, can leave the child with certain emotional difficulties such as anxiety or depression in the future, so it's very important to deal with it. It's also important to deal with it for the sake of your relationship with your partner.

You cannot respond to your partner in a concerned, loving way if you are depressed. Don't be Superman or Superwoman. Go and get help.

Who's complaining?

It might not be news to men that more than 80 per cent of the complaining in marriages is done by wives.

And it might not be news to women that even in successful marriages most of the things that couples argue about remain unresolved.

These findings have been arrived at by US psychologists John Gottman and his wife Julie Schwartz Gottman. Their research into marital harmony and disharmony has made them famous and, no doubt, rich.

Given the figures above, what hope is there for any marriage? The hope lies in this: according to the Gottmans the success or failure of a marriage does not depend on whether the couples fight. After all, fighting is one of the things couples do and there really is little point in getting upset over that fact in itself. What matters, the Gottmans would say, is how people fight and how good they are at making up afterwards.

This is where they introduce what they call the Four Horsemen of the Apocalypse. These four chaps generally herald chaos and destruction. They are not good to have around, especially in your marriage. The Gottmans use the term 'Four Horsemen of the Apocalypse' to describe four behaviours that, if they become a core part of the marriage, mean the marriage is at very high risk indeed of breaking up.

The Horsemen travel in pairs. The first two are *criticism* and *defensiveness*. The pattern is that she criticises harshly and he defends himself. This happens again and again. Communication suffers and nothing really changes.

If this persists, the next two Horsemen come clattering along. These are *contempt* and *stonewalling*. Criticism has changed to contempt and defensiveness to stonewalling. The prospect of meaningful communication has gone.

There was a time when people would have put up with this kind of thing for the rest of their lives. They had little real choice. In today's world, however, the chances are high that one or the other will look for a separation or divorce.

By the way, one of the great problems with contempt and stonewalling is that each partner develops a distorted view of what is going on. In other words, each partner sees the other person as solely responsible for everything that is bad about the marriage. Neither is able to see how they contribute to the likely breakdown.

The Gottmans, accepting that criticism is part and parcel of any close human relationship, encourage those who wish to criticise their partners to avoid harshness in the way they begin the criticism. 'You really sicken me,' is a harsh opening, for example, and criticism introduced in that way will simply not be heard in any meaningful manner by the other person. As for the target of the criticism, usually the man, the Gottmans suggest that he look at some changes he could make rather than simply assuming that all the criticism is invalid.

They noted that couples with successful marriages manage to put their rows behind them reasonably quickly. They do not keep them going for weeks and months.

They found, too, that if the couple show their appreciation to each other as a matter of course during the marriage then the relationship has a much better chance of surviving the inevitable storms. This is not just a matter of flowers and chocolates. It might be listening to your partner's account of their day, smiling at your partner, sharing light moments or responding to your partner's attempts at conversation. These are all things that actually don't cost money at all.

However, if you have ever dealt with warring couples you will know that many couples are far, far beyond being able to do any of these things. They might look simplistic, but just try doing them when you and your partner have been at odds for years!

I suppose what the Gottmans are really talking about is applying tolerance and appreciation to each other. And you really, really, need to start doing that before things get so bad you can only communicate through the lawyers.

Now or later – how men and women differ over housework

Back when people lived in flats, a journalist colleague shared accommodation in Dublin with several other guys. Their procedure for dealing with the washing up was as follows. They bought the cheapest cups and plates they could get. At the end of each meal, all used articles went into the sink. There they stayed. The question of washing them did not arise.

When everything had been used up, a couple of the lads went off to the environs of Moore Street and bought a new supply of chipped plates, saucers and cups for next to nothing. The old, unwashed items went into the bin and the cycle began again with the new set.

This is the sort of thing that men are capable of doing. It is also the sort of thing that women are incapable of understanding, let alone doing. Women are in the unfortunate position of having their brains wired up in a way that makes them better than men at noticing details. That's why they are better at remembering the routes of car journeys, for instance. It is also why they will notice that a friend has altered her hair colouring by 0.001 per cent whereas men wouldn't notice if she dyed it green.

This has its disadvantages too, for both genders. The man has no problem watching television, reading his paper or playing with his laptop until 'later', even though the carpet needs vacuuming and the dishes need putting into the dishwasher. These environmental details do not impinge on him.

The woman cannot do this. The fluff on the carpet and the dishes in the sink stand out in stark relief. They squeak and gibber at her. They disturb her peace. She either has to deal with them or she has to harass her male partner into dealing with them – and that's why the female eye for detail is a nuisance to both genders.

Mind you, if men realised their partners were more likely to have sex with them when they shared in the housework, they might be sticking on the apron and getting out the vacuum cleaner more often. I'll come back to that later.

Housework is, I think, among the least favourite occupations of both men and women. When it comes to the men, I think we have to admit that we're a disgrace. Earlier this year, the Equal Opportunities Commission in Britain forecast that men will never do their fair share of housework. By contrast, it will only take 65 years for the number of women running FTSE 100 companies to equal the number of men at the top.

And this all seems to have something to do with marriage. Back in 1994, a researcher in the US found that married women did more housework than women who co-habit. Since then, nothing has changed. A new study of more than 17,000 people in 28 countries has found that co-habiting men do more housework than men who are married. So those 90,000+ Irish households in which people are co-habiting are probably a lot cleaner than the households of married couples.

There's probably less tension in them too – fewer rows about housework – and more sex. Alright, here's the sex thing. When US author Neil Chethik interviewed more than 300 men for his book *VoiceMale* he found that wives who were happier with the amount of housework their husbands were doing had sex with them more often. Other experts on gender differences and marriage have reported the same thing. The great thing is, Chethik found, the man doesn't even have to do 50 per cent of the housework. So long as the woman feels the man is doing his fair share, she is more likely to turn up the romance.

Nobody is suggesting that there is a deliberate calculation going on in the woman's head – it's just further proof that we humans are unaware of our motivations at least half the time.

So, guys, if you want more action in the bedroom, forget the flowers and chocolates – get out the duster instead.

Death of a father – an emotional earthquake

'But, you must know, your father lost a father;
That father lost, lost his ...'

The words are those of King Claudius as he attempts to deflect Hamlet's grief and rage at the death of his father whom Claudius has murdered.

They are not, I suppose, dissimilar to words that are spoken in real life as people attempt to console those who are grieving. But the death of a father cannot be dismissed with words like that. A father is a larger-than-life figure to his children, even to his adult children. His death is an emotional shock that, in most cases, becomes one of the unforgettable markers along the road of their lives.

Indeed, judging by the death of my own father more than twenty years ago, and from conversations I have had with people in similar situations, the death comes as a shock even if it is long expected and even if it is a relief to the person who dies.

It is as though an earthquake has occurred in one's emotional life. There can be a sense that this event has been so profound that you cannot drift along in the old way but must do something of significance with your own life. That sentiment can put the bereaved adult child on the road to profound change before it fades away.

The father is an ordinary man. He has the strengths and weaknesses of ordinary men. However, unless you have been desperately unlucky, your father's strengths will seem quite extraordinary and his weaknesses relatively insignificant or, if not insignificant, forgivable.

In a sense, we never stop looking at our fathers through the eyes of the child to whom he is an almost magical figure of great power. I suppose that's something that we fathers have going for us. We may feel dissatisfied with ourselves or only too aware of our shortcomings, but our children, generally, know nothing of this.

Somebody once said that if you want to lead a good life you should try to be the person your dog thinks you are. Well, that would certainly be more achievable than being the person your children think you are! (I have to confess, though, that even being the person my dog thinks I am would be a tall order for me.)

These thoughts were spurred by an entry in *Newton's Laws*, an Irish blog by Paul Newton, in which he wrote movingly about the death of his father:

> Everyone leaves a legacy, some people leave millions of pounds, some leave heartache and sorrow, my father left neither of those, he left something far more valuable; he left me the things he valued greatly, the virtue of strength, the importance of gentleness, the necessity for dignity, the power of passion.

> He was my port of last resort, and he would bail me out, we got through those times and grew closer because of them, and when he died I knew I owed him nothing except to keep his values intact, to live a life that gave of my best, that left it out there on the field, a life that would allow me to live at peace with myself.

Are sentiments like these felt to the same extent, I wonder, by those whose father has never lived in the family home as by children of conventional families? I think the answer is yes, if the father is interested and involved. Revering our parents, even when we give them trouble, seems to be an inherent part of us. Social workers encounter children who revere parents who have treated them abominably.

And what gift can we fathers give to our children? I suppose we could at least make the attempt to be the person they think we are even though we know we will fall short. Perhaps we might also bear in mind that there is somebody whom the children want to impress and that's us. Maybe we should take care, now and then, to give them back some of the admiration that we get from them almost by default.

Paying the price for the lack of an emotional education

How much, I wonder, does the lack of an emotional education contribute to depression among young men?

By emotional education I mean an education in, among other things, how to cope with the emotional pain that accompanies the major disappointments we all experience from time to time in life.

I am specifically concerned with young men in this regard because young women get a sort of rudimentary emotional education from each other, since they talk more freely about feelings and relationship problems. It's far from a perfect system, as the level of self-harm among young women suggests, but it is better than nothing.

The whole concept of an emotional education is one we have never really embraced. Thirty or forty years ago students learned something in Christian doctrine classes about dealing with life's problems. Whatever we may think today about what they were taught, they were at least given some framework within which to address the vicissitudes of life.

Young men were also probably more inclined at that time to listen to the advice of older men on handling life's challenges. In the 1960s and 1970s the cult of youth was beginning to grow and the status of older people was already falling. Nevertheless, an older person who had gained experience of life and who had fashioned a philosophy out of that experience might have got a better hearing then than now.

Work at the time was more physical than it is today. We know that physical exercise helps to combat depression – exercise has been officially listed in the UK as a treatment for depression. So a hard day's physical work, of the sort that we would probably all run away from today, was good for people's mental health. I wonder if this has anything to do with the belief among those who study the history of such things that there is more depression today than there was early in the twentieth century when life was physically much harder than it is now?

Does this leave us in a situation in which young men are at sea when it comes to knowing how to be with their feelings? Is this why young men, and, of course, many young women, use alcohol to a degree which seems to have less to do with enjoyment than deadening their experience of their own emotions?

Alcohol and drugs will work for a while when it comes to coping with pain or with avoiding life's difficulties. Unfortunately, however, they do not go on working indefinitely. There are problems that you cannot fix with booze or with driving too fast. Some of these problems may even be caused by the booze or drugs themselves. You can get through a lot of years in a cannabis haze until the day you realise you have spent a lot of years getting nowhere and that you do not know what to do about it.

It is when young men hit this particular wall that they are in real trouble. And perhaps it is in this area that we need to think of intervening to boost their emotional health and to build their resilience in the face of the challenges thrown up by life.

Is there a place in the education system for a determined effort to provide an emotional education for young men and young women? Might it not pay off wonderfully in reducing damage to young minds and bodies?

It would not necessarily be an easy thing to devise and implement such a programme of emotional education in the schools. It would raise fears and would cost money. Anybody who remembers the campaign of opposition to the introduction of the Stay Safe programme for primary schools will be aware of just how controversial such a valuable and well-meaning move can be. Thankfully, the programme was eventually introduced and may have saved many a child from abuse.

If we want to improve the emotional health of young men and, indeed, young women, then perhaps we need, as a society, to do more educating and less preaching.

Snorers and sheet-stealers

So what's your partner like in bed? Does she kick and tear the sheets off you and leave you exhausted the next morning? Or does she complain that she can't get a night's sleep with your carry-on?

You could write a book about what goes on in bed, and somebody has. Sociologist Paul Rosenblatt has written a rather scholarly book on the subject called *Two in a Bed: The Social System of Couple Bed Sharing*, published by the State University of New York Press, no less.

Most couples value the bed for the intimacy and because it's where they talk over the events of the day, he found. People mentioned sex too, but not all that much.

But it's not all plain sailing. There is the issue of people stealing their partner's sheets during the night and differences over room temperature and whether windows should be kept open or shut. Then there is the question of snoring. As a snorer I am, personally, on the side of persons with this affliction. It is particularly annoying when people wake you up in the middle of the night to complain that you've been keeping them awake with your snoring – when you know you are innocent because, after all, you didn't wake yourself up. Still, I've compromised by buying large quantities of anti-snoring remedies. If my wife could get over the snoring thing I reckon we could afford an extra holiday in the sun.

According to the book, common sources of conflict in the bedroom are arguments over one partner watching TV or listening to the radio while the other is trying to sleep. And there is the insomniac who keeps the other partner awake by tossing and turning all night so that they are both exhausted by the morning.

In the twenty-first century, the couple's bed is increasingly invaded by gadgets, a source of conflict for some and of togetherness for others. The thoroughly wired-up couple lie side by side propped up on their pillows bebo-ing away on their respective laptops. Who are they bebo-ing and why? Is it considered acceptable for one partner to investigate what's on the other partner's screen? Is tapping away on your laptop more or less acceptable than fingering your BlackBerry? We need an etiquette to cover this historically unprecedented situation.

Traditionalist partners object to this. The bed is a place for comfort, unwinding, spooning and talking things over, they argue. It is not a place for blogging or for working on your department's projections for the next three months. I don't blog in bed because the wireless broadband signal doesn't reach the bedroom, despite what the man in the shop promised, so I have no idea how these arguments play out.

Despite all these differences and niggles, most people like to sleep with their partner for the comfort and intimacy. That's why deciding to sleep in the spare room or on the livingroom sofa for any prolonged period of time represents a serious breach in a marriage. It doesn't matter very much if it just happens now and again as a form of sulking, but it is not good news if it goes on and on because the couple have grown cold towards each other. Somehow sleeping apart in this way symbolises a loss of closeness that cannot be replicated outside the bedroom.

The closeness signified by the marital bed is, no doubt, behind the continuing speculation and even argument over Shakespeare's will in which he left his second-best bed to his wife. In fairness to the Bard, it is said that the best bed was generally reserved for guests at the time and that what he left her was the marital bed in which they had shared comfort and intimacy.

So appreciate your bed. It is more than a place for sleep. It is, in many ways, the place in which the relationship lives and breathes – and sometimes snores.

Separate beds more fun?

Counsellors can get a little too pious for their own good sometimes, especially when they put pen to paper. I am no exception to this rule. Last week, when writing about couples sleeping in separate beds, I intoned that 'sleeping apart in this way symbolises a loss of closeness which cannot be replicated outside the bedroom'.

I take it all back! What changed my mind was this response from Patricia, a lady given to jumping out of wardrobes and, I suspect, swinging from lampshades and all thanks to separate rooms:

> Having shared a bed with my husband for the first fifteen years of our marriage, I never, despite every effort on his part, got a night's sleep – the usual reasons: snoring, breaking wind, kicking, talking in his sleep, taking the duvet etc.
>
> We came to an arrangement, after a long discussion, to have separate rooms. Now we both sleep when we want, read when we want, look at television, listen to the radio – no fighting over the station, snore, fart, eat, drink, go to bed when we want, not having a light suddenly put on etc.
>
> We also have a very intimate relationship and surprise each other in our little funny ways – jumping out of wardrobes etc. – a lot more exciting than what we had when we shared a bed.
>
> Think again and tell all those suffering women, and a few men perhaps, that life/relationships go on when you take the step towards separate bedrooms. Encourage them to give it a try and I bet any money they will not go back to the old ways.
>
> I firmly believe you get what you put into a relationship and everyone has to work to keep the fun and intimacy alive.

Well, in the light of that I have to admit that my rather stuffy contention that sleeping apart 'symbolises a loss of closeness' has had to bite the dust. Do I hear the sound of hammer and saw as bedroom extensions are built all across the land? Yes, I suspect I do! And don't forget to put in good, big wardrobes for jumping out of.

Last week's article also mentions snoring as a source of conflict between couples sharing the same bed. However, Mary Gilroy Johnson, whose voice is familiar to listeners to Radio Kerry's Sunday morning *Horizons* show, writes to say that to her as a child snoring became the most comforting sound in the world. Later on, it was a godsend when she was sneaking into the house late from dances.

> My late father was a terrific snorer and my late mother a light sleeper. They shared a bed and it is a tribute to love and romance that Mum rarely had a decent night's sleep with her husband blissfully snoring his head off beside her.

> We children loved the snoring. It was the most comforting sound if you woke up from a nightmare … first the nightmare, then the sudden waking … the silence and the dark and then the blissful sound reverberating through the house. You were safe and sound and put yourself back to sleep to the rhythm of the snores.

> The snoring was most useful during the length of my misspent youth in which my father was alive. Sneak in the front door … listen … then when the snoring started take a few steps of the stairs, pause in the snoring, pause on the stairs and so on until you were safely in bed. Mother could never hear anything while father was snoring.

> To this day to me it is one of the most comforting sounds in the world … a lullaby in fact.

Take that, all you anti-snorers out there.

But back to separate bedrooms. When I suggested to Patricia that to have one's spouse lepping out of the wardrobe when you're on the way to bed might be disturbing, she replied:

> Believe me when I tell you women like surprises in the bedroom. No matter what age, spice up your relationship, but unless you have a very secure light fitting don't swing from the shade!!!

Hmmmmm. Separate rooms anybody?

She's right, you're not the one she married – but neither is she

If your wife has been telling you lately that you're not the man she married, she's probably right. The thing is, she's probably not the woman you married either.

Marriages go through stages. These stages also apply to those long-term, live-in relationships that are marriages in everything except the law.

For most of us, the romantic stage marks the start of a long-term relationship. That stage, however, is followed by what could be called a power struggle between the two parties. That is in turn is followed by either the break up of the relationship or by an accommodation between the two people involved.

Let's look at an example. You know those ads where the girl feeds the guy ice cream from a spoon? They're both in a kind of half shadow and they're both wearing vests and they're both very sexy. So there they are, really happy and really into each other. That's the romantic stage and it ends with them getting married or moving in together.

Now each begins to pay more attention to the differences between them. Those endearing differences become really annoying. 'I hate the way you stick that spoon of ice cream in my mouth with all your germs, yeuuchh!' he says. 'You're such a wimp, you expect me to spoonfeed you all the time,' she replies.

She used to think his habit of leaving his clothes lying all over the place was a sign of a free spirit; now she thinks it's disgusting. He used to think her tidiness fetish was cute; now he thinks she's

PADRAIG O'MORAIN

an obsessive witch who's choking the life out of him. We have moved into the power struggle. Why can't you be more like me? Why can't you see everything my way? Why do you go on doing your stupid man/woman things despite the fact that you have my excellent example to guide you?

The power struggle can end in the destruction of the relationship. But it can end in other ways too. For instance, there can be a cold war in which the couple go through their whole lives living together but without really experiencing warmth towards each other ever again. Or one can win and the other can lose, so that you have one partner who never disagrees with the other partner again. There is an awful silence imposed on one by the other. What a dreadful way to live!

One of the good ways it can end is in a sort of amused, mutual tolerance. Ah sure, that's the way she/he is. There's a mutual respect or tolerance there without the necessity to beat each other into a pulp for being different. Another good way for it to end is in mutual creativity, a mutual support for the development of the other person. Thus, we hear of partners supporting each other through career changes, studying and so on.

The good outcomes do not mean that there will be no fights in the future. It is more or less impossible for two human beings to live together permanently without having rows. We're just too darn ornery not to fight.

I mention this because people who have bought into the romantic version of love and marriage sometimes believe true love means no fighting. Well it doesn't: sharp disagreements are all part of the deal. So if you're in the doghouse – and how come it's always the guy who's in the doghouse? – it doesn't mean she doesn't love you or that it's time to call in the divorce lawyers.

Nor need you go around feeling guilty because the romantic stage is over: the romantic stage was always going to be over and be replaced by a stage that has the potential to be deeper and closer because it is more genuine.

Mind you, a little romance never hurts and be very sure you don't forget the anniversary – there's another thing, how come it's always up to the guy to remember the anniversary? – or it's back to the doghouse for you.

Mammy's boy

Are you a mammy's boy? Does your wife claim, as Princess Diana once famously did, that there are three persons in your marriage, only she doesn't mean Camilla – she means the mammy?

When you married, did you pop back to the mammy for your dinner every evening as soon as you came back from the honeymoon? Would the concept of not going to her for Sunday dinner be unthinkable?

When you were a child, would the mammy take the hot water bottle out of your sister's bed on a cold night to keep your feet warm? And if there was only enough money to send yourself or your sister to college, was it you that was sent?

If you are a mammy's boy and you marry, I suspect it will be to one of two kinds of women. The first is the kind who was reared to be with someone like you – namely a woman who will mind you. That should work if it is what you were both looking for and if you both remain happy with the choice. The second kind of woman is strong and independent who, for some reason best known only to Dr Freud, decided you were the man of her dreams. If that is who you married, then she may no longer be very happy with her situation. There is a fair chance that one day you will be back with the mammy while your ex-wife goes off to get a life.

Anybody who has ever had adolescent children knows one of the tasks of adolescence is to separate out from parents. It is a messy business, usually accompanied by much slamming of doors, thundering and stomping around the place. Still, it has to be done. If you are a mammy's boy who never actually separated out from your mother then your wife can feel herself

PADRAIG O'MORAIN

to be an outsider in a family made up of you, your mother and possibly your father as well.

If the marriage is to be a reasonably good one, the husband has to take the vital step of putting his wife in first place and leaving his parents' home, psychologically, for good. It's easier said than done. Some manage it and some do not.

I was led to these reflections after coming across the phrase 'mama's boy' in a book called *The Nonsexist Word Finder: A Dictionary of Gender-Free Usage* by Rosalie Maggio. That doesn't sound like the sort of book a person would want to spend time with but it turns out to be one of those volumes that can occupy hours when you should be doing something more important, like earning a living.

Ms Maggio's dictionary provides alternatives to words and phrases that could be regarded as sexist. On the topic of the mammy's boy, Ms Maggio expresses the view that this concept encourages many parents to deny their sons the warm nurturing they need for fear that they will turn into mammy's boys. Some of them spend their lives seeking that warmth, 'often in inappropriate ways'.

What really stopped me in my tracks was her dismissal of the word 'mammy'! Yes, shocking I know, especially if you are a mammy's boy yourself. The term 'mammy' should be avoided, she declares: 'This term is sexist (there is no parallel name for a man), racist and a stereotype that was probably always highly mythical.' I assume from her name that Ms Maggio is not Irish. Had she been so, I wonder would she have been so quick to dismiss the mammy?

And if you are ever tempted to describe your nearest and dearest, in your own mind, as a castrating bitch or a castrating woman, Ms Maggio advises you to 'avoid these expressions. They blame women for something that takes two to accomplish. It is not possible to castrate a secure, independent person; the man is not an anaesthetised patient in this type of surgery'. Well, no, I suppose not – unless, of course, it's the mammy who is doing the surgery.

Man in doghouse

Are you in the doghouse? The 'you' to whom I refer is, of course, a man. Women don't get put into the doghouse. It is a residence exclusively reserved for the male of the species.

Nor can men put each other in the doghouse unless, I suppose, they are in a gay relationship. With the aforementioned exception, the key to the doghouse is exclusively held by the woman in your life.

Chambers Dictionary describes the doghouse as 'a place of disgrace'. I am not sure they have captured the full flavour of the doghouse experience in that definition. Yes, when you are in the doghouse you are in disgrace for some lapse or misdemeanour. Usually you know what that lapse or misdemeanour is; sometimes you have absolutely no idea. Either way, you are in disgrace.

There is more than that going on, however. There is also a sort of cleansing process in train that is designed to make you fit for female company again. This cleansing process is a bit like money laundering in which dirty money is processed through a series of accounts to make it clean again. The doghouse process involves putting you through experiences such as silences, sighs, pursed lips and general indications that your welfare is of no interest to your partner.

When are you are let out of the doghouse you gradually become an acceptable human being again. Your sins are put to one side. You are entitled to take your place once more at the table of humanity.

It is a peculiar process and one that men seem to experience quite a lot. 'Are you in the doghouse?' I asked a man once. 'Are we ever out of it?' he replied. His attitude, I thought, was

PADRAIG O'MORAIN

somewhat pessimistic but certainly men must get used to the idea that they will be spending time in the doghouse during their one life on this earth.

There is a certain etiquette to being in the doghouse. For instance, it is important to maintain a respectful silence as if it does not matter to you at all that your partner is never going to speak to you again. You must also maintain a sort of dignified bearing while you are in the doghouse. You are not a man who shuffles or stumbles about the place. You are a man who knows his own importance and to whom dignity is everything.

Of course, you must display a supreme indifference to the question of whether your dinner is cooked for you or not. Your attitude must be that you are quite prepared to make your own dinner every day for the rest of your life if required. Perhaps you might even do a little bit of tidying or washing-up to demonstrate that you are entirely self-sufficient.

Being in the doghouse is not the worst thing that can happen. For instance, it is not as bad as being kicked out onto the street or being divorced. He who is in the doghouse will be let out of the doghouse – eventually.

That said, the doghouse is a tiring and unpleasant place in which to be. Women tell me that they also find the whole process to be tiring and unpleasant. And that is why I always think that a key skill in handling relationships between people living together is that of getting over a row quickly. Rows there will be – that is inevitable – but if you could have a rule that one or the other of you would try to make up within an hour or so of an average row you might not have to have the tiring doghouse experience.

Perhaps that is a counsel of perfection. It can be done some of the time but not all the time. We men must get used to the idea that we will be spending some time in the doghouse and not get too upset over it. After all, we love the women who put us there and they love us.

In the doghouse again

My piece about the male experience of being 'in the doghouse' has, I am afraid, annoyed some of my readers and I am now in the doghouse myself.

I suggested that being in the doghouse is an exclusively male experience. Men are put in the doghouse by their partners for our offences, real or imagined, for a day or two at a time.

Reader Ruth Stokes from Clonmel suggests that 'this is on a par with: "Black people do not get bullied. It is a situation exclusively reserved for white people." Absurd, untrue and offensive, in addition to promoting further discrimination, prejudice and injustice'. She adds:

> What you described as 'silences, sighs, pursed lips and general indications that your welfare is of no interest to your partner' are inflicted on many women by their male partners. The fact that the women who have spoken to you have not told you this does not mean that it is not happening. The fact that the men who have spoken to you may have said that they are victims of such ill-treatment does not mean that all men are victims nor does it mean that all women are bullies.

> As a reader of *The Irish Times* I expect accuracy and fairness in reporting and features – regardless of the gender, race, age, socioeconomic background or marital status of the writer.

Another reader, who does not wish to be identified, stated that women too, are subjected to sulking and silences from their men. These experiences, she said, are a great deal more distressing than I made out in my article. She objected to my use of stereotypes (I referred to the man in the doghouse affecting indifference as to whether he got his dinner or not) and to what she saw as my lame attempts at humour in relation to such a serious subject.

It seems to me that there is a distinction to be made between the sort of experience I described and the more serious behaviours to which my readers refer. I do not regard the experience of being in the doghouse as one of being bullied or as involving one person setting out to hurt another.

The doghouse experience, which I think is a normal part of all intimate relationships, involves one partner – usually the woman, in my opinion – affecting to withdraw her warmth and social support from the man for a period of hours or days. I say 'affecting to withdraw' because I do not believe this withdrawal is serious. If the man were in danger I have no doubt that the woman would step in to protect him.

There is a more serious level of conflict in which partners put each other through pain, psychological or physical, to punish them or to exert control over them to an extent which is damaging both to the other person and to the relationship. This can involve both emotional and physical pain, and sometimes both. That, I believe, is very different to the doghouse experience I described.

I know that Ms Stokes is unimpressed by this argument. Perceptions of what constitutes bullying vary depending on individual experiences and the social settings in which people find themselves, she pointed out when I put these points to her in an e-mail. She suggests that in my article I put forward 'generalisations not based on fact ... as if they were factual accounts'.

I can only respond that my views on the doghouse phenomenon were clearly my views. They do not purport to be based on research. When I use research as the basis of my articles I generally say so.

I believe there is a need to separate out the normal level of conflict in relationships from that which is unacceptable. I also believe, though I cannot produce a research study to back up my belief, that the experience of being in the doghouse is normal and nothing to write home about – whatever about writing articles about it in *The Irish Times*.

Are you a workplace bully?

Are you a workplace bully? Very few of us would admit, even to ourselves, that we bully people. Yet bullying in the workplace is so widespread that I suspect many bullies don't actually realise what they are doing.

Of course, there are those, both men and women, who bully deliberately. They may want to get a particular person out of a job so that they can be replaced by one of their cronies. Or a company may have a policy of bullying people who are out of favour but who don't want to leave.

However, it seems unlikely that all bullying can be explained in this way. Something else is going on. Some people bully because of their own insecurities – the victims of workplace bullies are normally people who are good at their jobs – and other people bully because they were reared to be rude and ignorant. Some are sociopaths, which is the latest word for psychopaths. And others, as I have said above, may not realise what they are doing.

So how would you know that you were engaging in behaviour that might be experienced by another person as bullying? Here is a checklist, based on some of the experiences of people who are bullied. If you recognise anything on it, consider whether you might be, unwittingly, behaving in a bullying way.

Let's start with 'slagging'. People slag other people all the time in the workplace and that's usually okay. But is there one person who is always the butt of your jokes or everybody else's jokes? It may all seem good-natured to you, but that person may be miserable at being endlessly mocked and made little of.

Is there one person whom you reprimand and criticise a lot? Do you criticise them in front of other people? Ask yourself whether you criticise this person for behaviour that you accept from other people. If you do, then you may well be bullying that person.

Is there somebody whose holiday requests you deny more often than you deny requests from other people? Is there somebody who says you roster them more often than anyone else for unpopular shifts?

Is there somebody in your department whom you regularly contact on business when they are on holidays or out sick? Perhaps the contact is justified some of the time – but this behaviour can often form part of a pattern of bullying.

Who, in your workplace, gets left out of group activities? Who never gets invited to the pub or the Christmas party? Who is left sitting alone in the canteen? Who does nobody ever address directly in the office?

Is there somebody to whom nobody talks because they once complained to management – unjustifiably in everyone's view – about being bullied? In effect, that person is now being bullied, whether or not they were bullied before.

Who is the person everyone has a laugh at, that people snigger about? What do you think it would feel like to be that person?

That these things are going on does not necessarily mean you are bullying someone – but it might. If you are a person who does not want to bully anyone, but who is doing some of the things mentioned in this article, then you can choose to stop doing them.

If you bully people to get them out of a job, then I don't suppose anything I say will stop you. And if you encourage a bullying culture in your workplace, then I definitely cannot stop you. One day this sort of behaviour will start to cost organisations money in compensation and when that day comes you will either change your ways or you will be out of a job.

If you would like more information about bullying in the workplace, take a look at the website of the Anti-Bullying Centre of Trinity College Dublin (www.abc.tcd.ie).

Protecting your mental health against workplace bullies

In the previous piece, I addressed readers who might, knowingly or unknowingly, be workplace bullies. But what if you are being bullied? How can you protect your mental health?

The effects of persistent bullying can continue long after victim or bully has moved to another job. Victims can become resentful and bitter. They can feel betrayed by employers and colleagues. Their confidence may be shattered.

That is why the people who leave their job after a prolonged period of bullying are at risk of remaining unemployed for a long time afterwards. They may find it hard to apply for jobs, to get through interviews or to go into a new workplace with any confidence that they will be treated well.

If you are bullied at work, how can you protect yourself against the emotional effects of what is going on?

The first thing you need to do is be careful of how you use your mind. You need to be aware of the message behind this quote from the South African anti-apartheid activist Steve Biko: 'The most potent weapon in the hands of the oppressor is the mind of the oppressed.'

Sometimes the bully only has to attack their victim now and then. The victim does the rest of the work by brooding and re-playing the incident over and over again while the bully sleeps peacefully. Therefore, if you are a victim of workplace bullying, it is very important to spot your tendency to endlessly replay these scenes. When you get into a replay, bring your attention back to whatever is going on around you right now – even if all that is going on is that you are breathing in and out. Also watch out for the tendency to endlessly fantasise about what you could or should have said and get your mind back into the present moment. You may have to do this many, many times a day, but it is worth the effort.

Talk to friends and relatives who are supportive and who will listen to you – but don't forget to talk about other things too. Talking helps but not if you are endlessly reliving the bullying.

Get exercise to burn off some of that stress. Sitting at home, going over every single detail of what has happened and of how you have been let down is far less healthy than taking a brisk walk.

You need to avoid comforting yourself by eating or drinking too much. Too much food or alcohol may bring some relief from the pain but ultimately it will simply leave you feeling bad about yourself.

If you have kids or a partner or friend be involved with them. Do normal things. Do not let this monster take over your life.

Finally, if your complaints and representations are getting you nowhere, give serious consideration to leaving the job. If your employer allows you to be abused like this, why continue working for them?

Watch out for the martyr syndrome in which you tell yourself you have to stay so that your colleagues won't have to experience bullying. Your destruction will do absolutely nothing to help your colleagues.

If you decide to leave, be wise about how you do it. Wait until you have another job to go to. The old saying that says it's easier to get the job if you are already have one is as true today as it ever was.

When you are bullied, somebody is taking away your control over your experience of your workplace. But there is something that you can still control – and that is taken care of your mental and physical health. Of course, you shouldn't have to take these measures but this is the hand you have been dealt – so play it as best you can for the sake of your own well-being.

And if you have never been bullied in the workplace consider yourself fortunate. If it ever does happen, remember that taking care of yourself is more important than taking care of the bully.

Just a brain thing

You know the scene: you are with your wife and she meets her best friend whom she hasn't seen for a couple of weeks.

'Oooooh!' the friend gushes. 'New shoes! They're gooooooooorgeous! Where did you get them?'

'Of course he,' the wife says, indicating you, 'didn't notice them at all. I could be wearing hobnail boots for all the difference it makes to him.'

Your futile efforts to pretend that you did in fact notice the shoes but didn't get around to mentioning them are dismissed. It's not just about shoes. It could be a new hairdo, only slightly different from the one she got before. It could be a new hair colour, differing by 0.01 per cent from the previous one. Never mind. The first woman who comes along will notice, be thrilled and enter into a conversation about the whole thing. And there you are saying to yourself, a new hairdo? I didn't know she got a new hairdo. Is that really a new colour?

Sometimes women get really unfair about this sort of thing. They close their eyes and they say:

'What colour are my eyes? Go on, tell me.'

And when you guess that they are brown, they say:

'There, you see? You pay no attention to me. You don't know a single thing about me.'

The point about all this is that these lapses are not due to indifference on the part of us men. They are due to variations in the way men's brains and women's brains are wired up. Women take in more detail than do men because their brains are structured to be very good at noticing details. Otherwise, they would find it just as hard as we do to notice dirty dishes, socks on the bedroom floor, new hairdos, new shoes or, God help us, new handbags.

Other variations, too, are caused by differences in brain structure and not by an unthinking and uncaring attitude on the part of us men. That area of a woman's brain that is linked to processing language happens to have more neurons packed in than does the corresponding part of a man's brain. That might explain why women talk so much. Or, as an article in *Scientific American* more diplomatically put it, it could explain 'women's enhanced performance in tests of verbal fluency'.

Women bond more than men. They put a higher value than men on conversations and actions that suggest togetherness. One of the primary chemicals that stimulate bonding is called oxytocin. Women's brains produce more oxytocin than do men's. So there's the woman talking and bonding madly while you'd rather be left alone with your thoughts – and at least some of that difference is down to oxytocin.

Differences in the way our brains are wired up come out in many other ways. Year-old babies will choose different types of toys depending on their gender. Girls are likely to choose dolls and boys to choose things they can throw or move, like cars. This difference is even found in male and female baby monkeys, who presumably have not been influenced by human society. If presented with a choice between looking at a human face and a mobile, day-old girls will spend more time looking at the human face and day-old boys at the mobile.

Getting from place to place also shows up inherent differences between men and women. Men tend to estimate distances and directions. Women tend to use known landmarks. Again, these variations seem to relate back to different structures in the brain.

What is the point in knowing all this? I think the point is that it enables us to understand the futility of undermining our relationships by criticising each other for perfectly natural differences. Many of the irritating flashpoints in our relationships have nothing to do with either of us being good or bad. They have everything to do with the way our brains are physically designed.

So a little tolerance is in order and a little humour and compromise on all sides. It's not deliberate. It's just a brain thing.

Anger, twits and bullies

Back in the days when Basil Fawlty mismanaged Fawlty Towers, his displays of anger were portrayed as ridiculous. When he verbally and physically abused his unfortunate Spanish waiter, we laughed – but we laughed at Basil.

Would his anger be portrayed in such a negative light if *Fawlty Towers* was written today? Today, TV chef Gordon Ramsay is feted and famous for his angry outbursts. I shudder to think of how many budding Little Caesars are eagerly absorbing Gordon's management style.

And yet, despite the current glorification of anger, I expect most of us can remember angry outbursts we regret. Excessive expressions of anger are bad for relationships, are a source of bullying in the workplace and are damaging to people's health.

A recently completed study of 670 military veterans in the US found that over a period of eight years, the men with the highest levels of hostility and anger suffered more rapid declines in their lung functioning than their less angry colleagues. The decline was greatest in the angriest men. It would take further research to clarify whether the hostility caused the decline in lung function or whether it was the other way around.

This and other links between anger and ill health suggest that being angry is not the good thing that some angry people make it out to be. Indeed there is reason to believe that outbursts simply stir up the anger and keep it simmering instead of getting rid of it. If you have something to say to a partner or colleague, it is a great deal better to say it clearly and without harshness than to shout abuse at them. Once you accept that excessive expressions of anger create more problems than they solve in home and work relationships and in your health, you're on your way to doing something about it.

But what? I think the first thing that needs to be done is to recognise that expressions of anger often follow a period of angry thinking. You might be thinking angry thoughts about something that happened thirty years ago or about something you heard on the radio thirty seconds ago. Either way, if your thoughts are angry, you are far more likely to lash out at the people around you. So be vigilant about the sort of thinking that goes on in your head. Once you spot the angry thoughts, get yourself out of your head and into the present moment by just noticing what's happening around you, what you're hearing and seeing and so on.

The second thing that may help is to become familiar with a phrase that is used by members of the international self-help organisation, Recovery Inc: people do things *that* annoy me not *to* annoy me. We get far more angry about, say, somebody cutting in front of us in traffic or somebody not coming over quickly enough to serve us in the shop if we think they are actually setting out to annoy us. It is the assumption that the other person is acting intentionally that ramps up the anger. There's no denying that the person is behaving annoyingly – but annoying you in particular is probably the furthest thing from their minds. Try it out: people do things *that* annoy me not *to* annoy me.

If your angry outbursts come so fast you don't even have the time to do what is outlined here, try to spot the physical changes that tell you an outburst is on the way. You might notice a rise in your body temperature, for example, or a tension in your head or chest. By becoming aware of these physical signals, you can buy time to apply these techniques.

These methods are similar to the traditional piece of advice to count to ten before responding to provocation. It is as good a piece of advice today as it ever was. I wish Gordon Ramsay and some of the twits who are absorbing all the wrong lessons from him would learn to apply it.

Social contact keeps us healthy; isolation makes us sick

In a society that seems to have become increasingly 'individualised', the risk of social isolation has almost certainly increased. That is particularly bad news if you are a man. There is a stack of evidence that being socially isolated damages men's health. However, there are also clues as to how this damage might be counteracted.

In the latest American research, thousands of men and women were asked about their social contacts. Social contacts included spouses, relatives, friends and religious or other groups. They then underwent blood tests to enable researchers to measure the concentration in their blood of markers indicating inflammation. Inflammation is thought to enable white blood cells to attach themselves to the sides of veins and arteries, leading to atherosclerosis with an elevated risk of heart trouble. What the study found was that the most socially isolated men had the highest inflammation and the most socially connected men had the lowest. In women, social isolation or connection made no difference.

European researchers have also found that deaths from stroke and heart disease occur at a higher rate in unmarried men than in men who are married. Again, in women, being married or unmarried seems to make little difference.

One British study even found that over a particular seven-year period single men were at greater risk of dying than smokers. This led one researcher to suggest that single men who smoke should get married as quickly as they can to counteract the health dangers of smoking. By the way, this wouldn't work for very long because the lifetime risk from smoking is far higher than it is over a seven-year period.

So what's going on? Researchers in the American study suggested that socially isolated men probably have less healthy lifestyles than those who are socially connected. They also suggested that people who are isolated are more likely to be stressed or depressed than those who are not. Stress and depression also seem to play a role in ill health.

Why are the findings for women different? The researchers suggested that the quality of women's relationships could be the vital factor here. Even socially isolated women, in such contacts as they have, are more likely to confide in someone than are single men, they suggested.

Confiding in someone may make all the difference to their levels of stress or depression, they suggest, and this makes women healthier. Married men, researchers point out, can confide in their wives. Single men often confide in no one.

There is also an old Swedish study that found people with social networks were less likely to develop dementia in old age than people who were isolated. Here, too, the quality of relationships seemed to be the vital factor. It wasn't necessary to see people every day or be surrounded by people all the time to get this protective effect. The important thing was being in touch with people and feeling you were part of a network.

These findings about the quality of relationships provide a clue as to how socially isolated men can protect their health: if there is someone you can confide in, even if you don't see them very often, then confide in them. Keeping in touch with relatives, friends and acquaintances can be crucial to the quality of your life. So can involvement with activities, organisations and so on.

There is something about us that needs contact with others even if we find other people a nuisance. Some people get around this by keeping in touch with networks of people on the internet, people with whom they may never meet but to whom they can tell their hopes, fears, worries, views and memories. I have never seen a study of the mental health benefits of such electronic contact but I suspect it has a value – so long as you are not shutting yourself off from flesh and blood people in your own environment to pursue it.

So the key finding from this research, especially for men, is: keep in touch, it could save your life.

Sexual abuse – making children blame themselves

The abuse of children can have serious long-term effects, as we know. Some of these effects are not often talked about but need to be talked about.

These include the decision by some abuse victims never to have children themselves for fear they will repeat the abuse, the belief that there was something about them in particular that attracted the abuser and a weight of guilt arising from having felt physical pleasure at some stages of the abuse.

By 'abuse' I mean neglect or physical, emotional or sexual abuse. Some men and women who suffered such abuse as children decide they will never marry or that, if they do, they will never have children. Their fear is that they would inevitably end up abusing their children in the way that they themselves were abused.

But it isn't so. Yes, it appears that an abused child is more likely to commit an offence as an adult than a child who was not abused. That, however, applies to a minority. Many people who were abused as children go on to be good, decent and loving parents to their own children. Indeed, I expect it is those who are most worried about repeating the cycle of abuse who are least likely to do so – because they are on their guard against it.

One of the nastier tactics of the child abuser is to induce guilt in the victim. This guilt can then go on to affect the victim's view of himself or herself for years. For example, a boy abused by a man may be told, or may conclude on his own, that there was something in particular about him that attracted men. As a result the boy can feel guilt because there is something 'wrong' with him.

He can also experience confusion about his own sexuality. Similarly, a girl abused by a man can wrongly conclude that she is particularly attractive to men, that somehow she is partly responsible for what happened and she may engage in various self-destructive behaviours.

What has actually happened, in both cases, is that the child was abused by a paedophile or by one of that small minority of men who are not paedophiles but who are willing to exploit children if they think they can get away with it. There was nothing particular or special about either of these children that attracted the abuser. Sadly, they were just children that could be exploited.

Most distressingly of all, people who suffered abuse are sometimes haunted as adults by a memory of having obtained a degree of physical pleasure from the abuse. Indeed the abuser may well have used this fact to try to make the child, especially an older child, assume the guilt about what went on. But the pleasure, if there was any, was simply a result of the biological way we are made and in no way condones the abuse of a child by an adult.

This can more easily be understood by looking at a non-sexual example: if someone was to kidnap you, lock you in a room and give you nothing to eat but a bar of chocolate, the chocolate would taste sweet. That doesn't mean it was alright to lock you in the room or that you wanted to be there: it just means we are biologically constructed so that chocolate tastes sweet, that's all. The experience of being kidnapped and held prisoner will still be damaging and traumatising. Similarly any experience of biological pleasure by a child who is being abused does not reduce by an iota the guilt of the abuser. In my opinion it actually increases that guilt by adding to the emotional pain of the child. The child remains innocent of any complicity in what is happening.

If you are an adult who was abused as a child and if you carry any of these forms of guilt around with you, try to realise that the guilt is a continuing part of the abuse and that it belongs to only one person – the abuser.

The impostor in the mirror

Do you see an impostor when you look in the mirror? You'd be surprised how many people do.

Most of us adopt or are thrust into roles in life that we think we are not up to. Other people might say you're great at your job or you're a great parent or a great partner, but they are looking at you from the outside. You are looking at yourself from the inside and you 'know' you are none of these things. What's more, you think, if other people knew you as well as you know yourself, they would agree with your unspoken opinion.

The so-called impostor phenomenon was first described in the late 1970s. Then, it referred to young women who were doing well in managerial and executive jobs in the workplace but could not give themselves credit for their own ability. They saw themselves as succeeding either because they were lucky or because they worked harder than anybody else – but not because they were intrinsically good at what they did. Subsequent research has shown that the term can be applied equally to men.

The odd thing about the impostor phenomenon is that it seems to affect people who are genuinely successful rather than people who fail. The 'impostor' may gain promotions, may be praised by colleagues, may be in demand among customers yet her or she feels like a fake.

Instead of basking in this praise and approval, the affected person lives in fear of being found out.

Another curious thing about people who feel like impostors is that they are less likely than others to behave like real impostors. For example, a study of college students found that those who felt like impostors were less likely than other students to cheat.

'Impostors' seem to dread the arrival of the day when their work will be judged, so they have developed ways to put off the evil hour. One is to put off starting tasks for as long as possible, always completing them just before the deadline. The other is to start work on a project long before everyone else, perhaps dragging out the preparations interminably and continuing to work beyond the point at which others are finished.

What's the payoff for these strategies? The first – putting the work off until the deadline is nigh, as I have done with this article – allows the 'impostor' to say the work was so rushed it was pure luck that it was any good. This neatly avoids the question of whether the person is inherently good at the job.

The strategy of working interminably on the project allows the 'impostor' to assert that anybody who put in this amount of work would be bound to succeed – again, the 'impostor' avoids the issue of his or her personal qualities.

Research on the impostor phenomenon has mainly concerned itself with the workplace and with college studies. However, I have no doubt that it applies also to relationships. The person who cannot take a compliment may be an example of someone who feels like an impostor.

My own phrase for this is 'the ah shure syndrome'. 'Aren't you really marvellous to have rescued your aunt from that burning building?' 'Ah shure, I was heading in the direction of the door anyway and she just kind of clung on to me.'

If you feel like an impostor and someone expresses love and admiration for you, you will conclude instantly that they don't know what they are talking about. And you will make sure they don't get close enough to find out what you are really like.

You believe that if they find out what you are really like, they will no longer admire or love you. To avoid this fate you may have rows with people when they get too close. Indeed, you may even walk away from them altogether.

It's a painful phenomenon and one that may be more prevalent at home and at work than we realise. I think it is also very difficult to get rid of, but awareness is the first step to reducing its influence on our lives.

Drinking to dull the pain

How many Irishmen use drink as a painkiller and not for enjoyment? Could it even be said that we get less enjoyment out of our drinking than do men in other European countries? It's a strange thought, given our reputation as big drinkers, yet it is likely that other nations enjoy a drink more than we do.

These thoughts are prompted by a piece of research from Cork University Hospital, published in the *Irish Medical Journal*. Most striking in that research was the finding that of those men who attended the emergency department and who were very drunk, half had also taken large amounts of medication in an attempt to harm themselves. That's a surprising figure but it is supported by other studies that have shown a link between excessive drinking and deliberate self-harm.

Oddly enough, if you looked at daily average consumption only, you would imagine we were restrained when it came to the drink. A table included in the study shows that just 1.6 per cent of men in Ireland drink every day (or at least admit to it). By contrast, 12 per cent of German men drink every day. However, when you look at binge drinking the picture changes completely: 48 per cent of Irishmen binge drink at least once a week, while only 9 per cent of German men do so. Indeed out of every 100 drinking sessions, Irishmen binge on 58 occasions and German men on 13.

The finding that half of the very drunk men surveyed in the emergency department at CUH had tried to harm themselves is supported by research done at Navan hospital in 2001. That research found that half of those patients who had taken a drug overdose also had an alcohol dependency.

Somewhere along the line the connection between pleasure and drinking has got lost. Remember the debate that led up to the liberalising of licensing hours? Those in favour, including myself, believed we would learn to drink slowly and enjoyably as people do on the Continent. There would be no more stacking up the pints just before closing time. Well, we all know what happened – we drank more and more and more.

In the ten years between 1989 and 1999, the consumption of alcohol per capita in Ireland rose by 41 per cent. We have all heard that statistic before, but it still astonishes me. Not everybody drinks or binge drinks, so that figure means that those who drink heavily and who binge are really drinking enormous quantities. This, in turn, suggests that there is an awful lot of emotional pain out there and that we are not dealing with it in an effective way.

I would suggest there is a case for ensuring that people who present at emergency departments with drink problems be given at least one session of counselling before they leave the department, even if it is just one brief session. There is some evidence from abroad that such counselling actually has an effect and that it encourages some people to take a more sensible approach to life's problems.

That would be a tiny step forward in dealing with this huge issue. Still, I am not optimistic that even that will happen. We are not good at providing resources for dealing with alcohol-related problems. Let's face it: we have enough problems to fill a clinic in every parish in the country. Yet people are routinely patched up in hospitals and then sent off without any special intervention to help them stop destroying their lives.

I suppose most people who binge drink fool themselves into believing they are enjoying themselves, but I am convinced that a point comes for most when they cannot fool themselves any longer.

If we as a nation could find a better way to handle our pain, perhaps we could quit binging and start to enjoy our drink for a change.

From the two of us to mammy and daddy

When a class from one of the local schools visited the zoo the other day, the main object of interest was the baby gorilla. My informants told me they could not see much of the baby because the mother was holding onto it very tightly. The father, I was told, was only allowed to approach when the mother beckoned him.

I bet there are few fathers reading this who can empathise with that experience. Human fathers sometimes feel cut out of many aspects of the rearing of a child, especially the firstborn, because of the mother's fiercely protective attitude.

She may suspect that if she lets the father pick it up, the baby will break. Or perhaps she fears the father will teach her baby bad habits like drinking and gambling. Either way, some fathers feel they are being kept literally at arm's length from the baby. Like their counterpart in the zoo, they are outside the inner circle.

The birth of the first baby has long been recognised as a potential time of challenge to the relationship between a couple. When they got married they may have been so madly in love with each other that, as the Bible puts it, the two became one. But when baby comes along it is a question no more of one or two but of three. And three, as we all know, is a crowd.

Not only is there now the third person in the household but this particular third person happens to be the most demanding one there. As a result, the new parents suddenly find they have little time or energy for each other.

. Of course, it makes perfect sense that the parents' attention should be directed towards the demanding but quite helpless creature who has entered their lives. Trouble begins when they forget to switch some of their attention back to each other. As time passes it is terribly easy to fall so far into the role of parents that the two lovers who decided to spend their lives together fade out of the picture. They may even start to call each other 'mammy' and 'daddy' as every meal, outing and holiday is built around the kids.

That is why some relationship counsellors encourage couples to go out on dates with each other minus the kids. Doing the things they used to do before the kids came along can reawaken two personalities who used to have fun together once upon a time. This is by no means the whole answer when a marriage gets into trouble but it can contribute a lot towards a solution. Some counsellors even suggest that the parents refuse to tell the kids where they go on these special dates. That's a way of emphasising to all concerned that they are a couple in their own right and not simply an extension of their children.

The key point, whatever they tell the kids, is that if the parents begin to go out as a couple again they can start to rediscover some of the feelings they had when they were courting. Now, by going out I mean going and doing things that interest and engage them, whether that's the races, a movie or a stroll in the park. We have all seen the bored married couples sitting in the pub with nothing to say to each other and it's a fate to be avoided.

Retaining their identity as a couple is something parents have to work on quite deliberately after Junior joins the family. You wouldn't think people would have to work on having fun but they do. If they don't round up babysitters and make time for each other, they may open their eyes one day and realise they've missed about two decades of life outside the home.

So what about that poor old gorilla dad down in the zoo? I think he would be very wise to work on the missus to hand Junior over to a babysitter now and then and go out for a quiet, romantic banana and a moonlight scratch.

Facing the inevitable – or not

A man in his seventies who spent most of his life in the practice of Zen Buddhism recalled an encounter concerning death.

It had occurred many decades previously when he was training under the eye of an old-style Zen master. He had been contemplating the subject of death and had become rather comfortable with it, thanks to many hours of meditation.

Foolishly, he informed his Zen master that he no longer feared death. The master responded by jumping on top of him – they did that sort of thing in those days – and began to strangle him.

This went on until the student had almost lost consciousness. Luckily, he had previously spent some years at sea and had learned how to take care of himself. He managed to land a punch on the jaw of the master and free himself.

When he regained his breath, he berated the master for almost killing him.

'But,' the Zen master replied, 'I thought you told me you had lost your fear of death?'

I presume the Zen master was trying to convey, in a way which would be barred by health and safety regulations nowadays, that if you say you have lost your fear of dying you are probably fooling yourself and anybody who believes you.

The dread of death seems to be common to people in Western cultures but this isn't always so elsewhere. There's a tribe in Micronesia in the Pacific Ocean that believes that everyone dies at forty. Even if, after reaching forty, you are walking, breathing and talking, you are still, essentially, dead. I apologise, by the way, to anybody who is staring down the barrel of the Big Four-O, but do remember that this is Micronesia we're talking about.

Far from struggling against the idea, people over forty seem to see the whole thing as a form of retirement. For instance, they don't work as hard anymore. After all, they're dead. What do you expect?

This acceptance of death and dying is found in many Buddhist traditions, too. Indeed, in those traditions in which there is a belief in reincarnation, the ambition is to reach a point at which you can finally die and don't have to be reincarnated anymore. That's an attitude most of us in the West find baffling, except when we're sitting in a traffic jam on the M50.

In facing our own death, there is the question, if we know it is coming, of what to say to those who are closest to us. Many men, I suspect, would be inclined to take a sort of stoic attitude to it and speak about it as little as possible. We would try to be good, strong men who are not going to upset other people by talking about our death. But, in fact, talking to our partner and children could help to ease the pain for everybody.

These thoughts were prompted by the Channel 4 series *The Mummy Diaries*, about how mothers facing death through terminal illness interact with their children. A key message of the series is that it brings comfort to children and partners if the mother talks to them about what is going to happen and if they gather up memories for after her death (these include letters to the children, reminiscences, advice for their future lives and so on). In other words, the whole family becomes involved in what is happening to one of its members.

It all seems so much healthier than denying that anything is going on at all and keeping everybody isolated in their own world of pain and fear.

Self-esteem at work and at home

What would you say your partner thinks of you? Does she contemplate you with a sigh of pleasure or a groan of exasperation? If you were spirited away by aliens would she miss you a little or a lot?

The answers you give to these questions may depend less on your knowledge of your partner than on your attitude towards yourself.

Among the more arresting findings from research into relationships is this: we tend to assume that our partner has the same opinion of us as we have of ourselves. So if you usually think you're a great fellow altogether, you will tend to assume that your partner also thinks you're a great fellow altogether. But if you think that, actually, you're a bit of a failure, then you will expect her to think the same.

A piece of research among couples in the US and Canada has produced a fascinating variation on this theme. The researchers found that if you're a person with low self-esteem and if you're having difficulties at work, you will assume your partner thinks worse of you than she does. You will assume this even if she thinks you're great and even if she doesn't know about your work problems. If your self-esteem is high this doesn't happen. You can have a bad day at work but it won't affect how you see your relationship with your partner.

What may be happening for people with low self-esteem is that they judge their goodness or badness, and their acceptability, according to how well they do at external things such as work. The concept of unconditional love has no reality for them. They may be receiving unconditional love from their partner but they don't really believe in it. It seems likely, then, that for a person whose self-esteem is low, a reprimand from the boss has a much wider effect than it would have on a person whose esteem is high.

What's the effect on the partner? It varies for men and women. If it is the female partner who has low self-esteem coupled with difficulties at work, the husband becomes more dissatisfied with the relationship. This may be because she is more likely to express her negative feelings than to hide them. If it is the man who has low self-esteem and problems at work, the woman's view of the relationship is unaffected. This may be due to men's tendency to hide their feelings.

It makes you wonder how many people spend long hours at the office, not because the job demands it, but because they would otherwise feel worthless? How many spend their holidays in a blizzard of phone calls and emails for the same reason? Could it be that in some part of their mind they believe this behaviour gives them worth in the eyes of their partner?

The scary point to come out of the research is the extent to which we live in our own little world without necessarily being in touch with reality. There we are, basing our assumptions about our partners on matters that have nothing to do with them at all and of which they may be unaware.

It's not just people with low self-esteem that are affected. If you have what some researchers call 'chronic high self-esteem' you may feel that your partner is absolutely delighted with you while she may already be googling 'divorce in Ireland' behind your back. Mind you, if I was offered the option of suffering from 'chronic high self-esteem' I'd take it – the divorce bid might come as a shock but at least I'd have my self-assurance to fall back on.

All this seems to suggest, then, that if you are unhappy with the relationship between yourself and your 'significant other' you might at least consider the possibility that the person you are really unhappy with is yourself.

Therefore, it's possible that the relationship you most need to improve is the one you're having with yourself. When you've figured out how to do that, be sure and let me know.

If you want a plump woman, marry her

There she is in the supermarket aisle, slim as a greyhound, choosing her little low-calorie meal for the evening. Before she has her 'dinner' she will go to the gym just to ensure that she stays nice and slim.

You, however, may prefer your women not to be all muscle and bone, but don't worry – all you have to do, the latest research suggests, is to marry her. It appears that marriage makes women gain weight. Is this because marriage makes them content and happy? I would like to think so but researchers have a way of spoiling the fun.

According to British obesity expert Dr David Haslam, writing recently in the *Lancet*, what happens is that living with a man means the woman has bigger meals than when she was single. Men need more energy and therefore need more food, says Dr Haslam – clearly a man after my own heart – so out go those little meals for one and in come the bigger portions. Treats will occasionally be indulged in, of course, and perhaps a bottle of wine will become part of the evening meal. The woman will gradually drop her trips to the gym in favour of a night in. Going out to restaurants will also help to put on the weight.

I'm afraid bigger meals are not the only thing your once trim, slim, super-fit babe is going to share with you. According to research by the University of Nottingham, married couples are also more likely to share conditions such as high blood pressure and excessive levels of cholesterol. Some of this, of course, could be related to those bigger meals. It could also be related to other lifestyle factors – both may be smokers or couch potatoes or may live in an atmosphere of stress and crisis.

The findings even apply to depression. If your partner suffers from depression then your chances of suffering from the condition are 70 per cent higher than normal. Researchers speculated that this might be because both partners are living in the same depressing social circumstances. They also speculated that people tending to be depressed might gravitate towards other people who also tend to be depressed.

It's all a bit grim isn't it? And yet death rates among married people are lower than death rates among their unmarried counterparts. Married men and women in any age group are less likely to die than those who are single. Perhaps this is because they have someone to listen to them and to give them emotional support. The married person, for example, has a spouse to nag them into going to the doctor if something appears to be wrong.

Typically, I suppose, it is the man who is nagged by the woman into going to see the doctor. From a male perspective, women seem ready to skip down to the doctor's surgery at the drop of a hat. A man, if he is unwell, may decide to give himself, oh, say, a year to see if he can get better on his own before bothering the GP about it.

So the nagging of one spouse by the other is probably helping to keep both of them alive. And if the nagging drives you to divorce, be aware of that your chances of dying early will increase substantially. Men who have been divorced drink more heavily than their married counterparts who have someone to keep an eye on them.

If they are sensible, the divorcees will return to buying those little meals for one and heading off to the gym every night before eating. Then they will become trim and slim again and can snap up a new partner and start over.

And this time around they could trade in the sofa for a membership for two at the gym, ban those big meals and live terribly healthy lives all round.

Mind you, I think I would rather be overweight and lazy and happy. But don't mind me. I am just a man.

What's in a gesture?

Marriage, as anyone who has spent more than a few days in that institution knows, provides opportunities for conflict and disagreement. But conflict and disagreement do not, in themselves, wreck marriages. If they did there would not be a marriage left intact on the planet.

When conflict and disagreement lead to the end of a marriage, it is not usually because the conflict occurred. It is more likely to result from what happened after the conflict. If the couple can recover from the conflict then, usually, all is well. That there will be more conflicts in the future is neither here nor there. Human beings are prone to fighting with each other, especially with those closest to them. In that respect we may be the dumbest species on earth.

Those who attempt to advise people on how to deal with conflict in marriage sometimes make what, in my opinion, is the mistake of focusing on avoiding conflict in the first place. Sometimes their suggestions are far removed from reality, especially from a man's point of view.

One standard piece of advice is to listen carefully while your partner is criticising you and then to repeat back the partner's criticism just to make sure you've got it right. So we men, having had our faults listed out by our enraged partners, are supposed to say something like the following: 'Let me just make sure that I've got it right, dear. I am a lazy, good-for-nothing hound who contributes nothing whatsoever to the running of the household, gives bad example to his children, a man whom no sensible, sane woman would put up with and who ought to be ashamed of himself in general for the rest of his life. Have I got that right and would you like to add anything to it, at all?' Can you see that happening? Neither can I.

The thing is, it is impossible to avoid conflict in a marriage and even if you tried to reflect back what the other person said you'd probably get it wrong and end up having a blazing row anyhow.

According to Dr John Gottmann, one of the best-known researchers on long-term relationships in the US, the key thing about conflict in marriage is what comes after the row. The marriages that last, he suggests, are those in which somebody makes a gesture of some kind after the row to repair the damage that was done.

What is that gesture? Well, it could be caring for somebody – asking them what they would like to eat, asking them if you can help them with something, making a joke (a very carefully chosen joke, I might add), complimenting the person and so on. That's a gesture. What about saying 'Sorry', you may ask? What about chocolates and flowers? Well, yes. But you know there are many people who find it really, really hard to say sorry and indeed there are people who are never going to say sorry no matter how sorry they actually feel. And chocolates and flowers bought at the wrong time may end up in the bin, if not someplace even worse.

For many of us men, who are not as comfortable talking about our feelings as women are, making some sort of gesture of the kind mentioned above is a way for us to signal that the conflict is at an end and that we want to move on. Women, usually, will know what the gesture means. Equally, if the woman makes the gesture it is important that the man recognises it and is able to accept it and move on.

So it doesn't really matter that you have rows. Nor does it matter that you have silences after rows. What matters is that one or the other of you is able to make some gesture of reconciliation and that the other is able to accept it and to get on with life.

So, think gestures. They count and they could save your marriage.

How grief kills relationships

How many marriages have broken up because men and women grieve differently?

The following is a generalisation but it's true often enough to be worth stating: women grieve on the outside and men grieve on the inside. While the woman cries, the man remains silent or does his crying out of her sight.

Is this why marriages are at a heightened risk of breaking up after the death of a child? The death of a child is every parent's nightmare. Other people assume that this unspeakable event will draw the couple so closely together that nothing could part them. The evidence, however, is that such a death can bring serious stresses to the relationship between the parents. Those of us who have never experienced it can hardly imagine the pain of a marriage break up in such circumstances. Yet it happens.

Because the man grieves silently and appears to be going about his day and his work as usual, he may seem to the woman to have got over the loss very quickly and to be unsympathetic to her suffering. Similarly, the man may be unsure as to what to do or say when the women is grieving so openly. He may feel that saying nothing is the best way to help her. She may feel abandoned. He may feel unable to share his grief for fear that doing so will make matters worse for her. The potential for a prolonged communications breakdown and for misunderstandings is obvious.

Fortunately, the death of a child is still a relatively rare event. Far more common are miscarriages and it seems to me that these have the potential to drive a couple apart because of different styles of grieving. Here too the woman is likely to grieve more openly than the man. To her, he may appear to have gone off to work after a day or two as if nothing has happened. Not only does he grieve on the inside but he may not know what to say to her about this event.

Matters can be made worse by a lack of support from family and friends. The experience of women who have spoken to me about this issue is that family and friends expect them to get over a miscarriage fairly quickly and to get on with their lives. This deprives the couple of an outlet for their feelings of grief.

A somewhat similar problem can arise following the death of a child or of any family member. Family and friends, unsure of what to say and not wanting to say the wrong thing, may avoid the grieving couple. It isn't that they actually make a decision to avoid them, it's just that whenever the idea of speaking to the couple or visiting them occurs, they put it off until tomorrow and tomorrow never comes. Even people who had been quite friendly with the couple may stop seeing them. This throws the couple back on their own resources and, if these resources are strained, the results can be quite serious.

Part of the solution is for couples to realise that their grieving styles are different and to accept this fact. Women need to be aware that the absence of open grieving does not mean that men get over these things any more quickly than women. Men need to take the trouble to let women know now and then that they are grieving. Each needs to support the other in their differing styles of grieving. Both need to realise that stresses in the marriage can be worsened by grief and to make allowances for this.

Family and friends can help by realising that the couple will need expressions of interest and sympathy for a very long time after the death. We sometimes seem to think that the pain is at its height around the time of the funeral and gradually lessens after that. Very often, however, the pain worsens after the mourners have gone away and the couple will need at least as much sympathy and support as before.

Ditching Mr Self-Sufficient

I am one of those men who won't ask for directions. I will drive doggedly from street to street for at least three-quarters of an hour before I give in and ask somebody for the information I need.

I am not alone in this. It is said to be characteristic of men that we will battle on and not ask for directions, even when this means going around in circles for ever and a day. At heart, we all want to be the strong, silent type who doesn't need help. Therefore, we don't ask for help until we have absolutely no option but to do so. So we try to 'tough out' illnesses, relationship problems and depression rather than admit that we need help. It's as if we think that asking for something – admitting that we actually have needs – is a sign of weakness.

On the contrary, asking for help can be very powerful. For example, if you want to get closer to somebody, ask them for help. At first glance, that doesn't make sense, but suppose you are in a relationship with somebody and some distance has grown between you. In that situation, asking her for help, even if you think you don't need help at the time, is a way of creating a deeper level of communication.

I'm talking here about pretty mundane things, like getting her opinion on how you might resolve two conflicting appointments or whether it would be a good idea for you to take the kids into town on Saturday. It doesn't have to be about the meaning of life. It's a way of saying, 'I need you, I'm not a self-sufficient person who doesn't need anybody. Please help me'. This approach will get you much further than being Mr Self-Sufficient.

Actually, the same thing applies in the world of work. If you need to deal with somebody in your organisation who is a bit of a curmudgeon and who, on first being asked for something, will bite your head off, try a different tack. Try saying, 'I have a bit of a problem, I'm not sure what to do. I wonder if you can help me?' Then explain what you want and quite often your curmudgeon will gladly give you what would have been refused if you had asked for it straight out.

Believe me, I've tried this and it works. Your curmudgeon responds well to a request for help because by asking for their help, you have acknowledged their power. You have allowed them to be generous. By the way, most of the curmudgeons I have worked with happen to have been male but this approach works with female curmudgeons too.

Good negotiators have no problem about asking. And here's an odd thing: guys in suits will go into a business negotiation and ask for this, that and the other and not feel in the least bashful about it. Ask them to go home and ask their wife for help and they go all shy. Of course, in business negotiations, both sides get to do lots of preening and strutting about. You won't get away with preening and strutting with the missus.

What that means, though, is that you have to be genuine with her. So if you need something, you have to abandon the strong, silent stance and come right out and say you need it. Is that why, in relationships, we so often go around acting as though we don't need anything? Do we fear that asking for what we need will make us appear weak?

To acknowledge that you actually have needs and that you are not incredibly self-sufficient won't make you a weakling. It will make you a human being and your partner in all likelihood will appreciate that fact and your relationships will grow stronger as a result.

Strong, silent types may look good in magazines and on the screen but they're not much fun to live with.

So ditch Mr Self-Sufficient and be a real human being with needs. It will get you further in the long run.

The emotional pain of male infertility

'I thought she was angry with me because I had let her down. I was unable to give her the most basic thing, a child. But she was angry with me because I was quiet.'

So writes Marc Jacobson, an infertile man, on the website of Resolve, the National Fertility Association (www.resolve.org) in the US. The same could be said by many men in Ireland. Infertility now affects one in seven couples in Europe. There are predictions that this proportion will rise over the next decade. In about 40 per cent of cases the man is infertile. In about 40 per cent of cases it is the woman who is infertile. In the remaining 20 per cent of cases both partners have problems that contribute to the infertility. Now the European Society for Human Reproduction and Embryology is suggesting that male infertility may be on the increase. This may be due, it suggests, to increased environmental pollution affecting the food chain and thereby affecting the quality and quantity of sperm produced by men. Infertility may also be on the increase because couples put off having children until later in life when they are less fertile.

I mention this because of the tendency of men to blame themselves for their infertility. It is important for men to realise that infertility is not their 'fault' at all any more than women's infertility is their 'fault'. But what I really want to say to men – as this column is aimed at men – is this: whatever happens as you deal with your infertility, make sure you keep the relationship with your partner as good as it can be. Whether you succeed in having a child or whether you don't, you will still need a good relationship with each other.

Here are some ways in which your reaction to your infertility can damage that relationship:

- Out of a sense of shame and hurt you avoid discussing the matter with your partner;
- Your anger at yourself comes out as irritability and anger against her;
- To maintain your sense of self-worth you throw yourself into other activities at work or elsewhere and give her too little attention;
- You avoid family gatherings where there are children and you expect her to avoid them too.

What most of these things amount to is the man isolating himself. This leaves the woman hurt and angry. As Marc Jacobson wrote in the quote above, the man then assumes she is angry because he cannot give her a child. In fact she is angry because he has withdrawn from her.

Fertility treatment constitutes one important danger point in the relationship. It is the woman who undergoes the procedure and the discomfort associated with it. The man will feel bad for putting her through this, as he sees it, and, again, is in danger of isolating or punishing himself in a way that actually punishes her. She loses his emotional support at the very time she needs it desperately: when she is going through the treatment or afterwards if the treatment has failed. In this situation, tension rises and minor, everyday matters become major rows. She thinks he is heartless or unconcerned. He, however, is acting out of hurt. If he would tell her that, it would represent a major step forward in saving the relationship. In the case of Marc Jacobson, he finally began to talk to his wife and to listen to her and they saved the relationship.

What all this means is that if you are a man who has an infertility problem, it is really important that you work on the relationship with your partner, not so that you will have a baby but because you will need each other whether you have a baby or not.

Above, I gave the address of the Resolve website, which has a good section for men. Here in Ireland we have the National Infertility Support and Information Group (www.infertilityireland.ie) and I would really urge you and your partner to contact them to get support from people who are going through what you are going through. Their telephone number is 1890 647 444.

Sauce for the goose?

I was wandering around a garden centre the other day when I spotted a little selection of plaques for sale with jokes on them about men. You know the sort of thing:

Most mornings I wake up feeling grumpy but sometimes I just let him sleep.

Or

Q. What do you call a man with half a brain?
A. Gifted.

Or

Q. What did God say after creating man?
A. I can do better.

I got to wondering why you don't see plaques like that with jokes about women on them in your friendly garden centre. Could it be that the emancipated sisters can dish it out but cannot take it? It is not that women do not like jokes, or even dirty jokes. I have seen some of the jokes they text each other and they would strip the paint off the walls.

I realise, I even applaud, the fact that women are getting their own back in the jokes department after many decades of tolerating stupid sexist jokes. Naturally they are retaliating, not by developing nice girlie jokes, but by making stupid sexist jokes about men.

Well, I am not going to turn around now and retell a bunch of sexist jokes about women. Still, in the spirit of the above, I thought I might bring to a wider public the following dozen hints and tips for women seeking to understand their men. I assure you that if women could just manage to observe this wisdom, life would be so much better for everybody.

Here they are:

Girls, please learn how to use a toilet seat. After you're finished, leave it up, not down.

Learn to live with the fact that we are not always thinking about you.

Don't ask us which pair of shoes goes best with your dress. We don't know and, more importantly, we don't care.

If you tell us about a problem and we give you a solution, don't start banging on about our lack of empathy. If you want someone to cry with you and to bang on endlessly about whatever it is, go out with the girls.

If we said something unpleasant to you six months ago and if we've already had the row about it, you are not allowed to bring it up again. We have served our sentence and we have paid our debt to society.

You can interpret our jokes in a way that makes you laugh or in a way that makes you angry. Kindly understand that what we meant was the first, not the second.

In those cases where you know best how to do something, please save us all a lot of trouble and do it yourself. We understand this means you are going to be a very busy woman but, hey, that's the price of perfection!

If you have something important to say, please condense it to a statement that can fit in between the commercials.

There is no need to demand that we keep telling you we love you. We told you the day we got married. What more do you want?

We don't know the difference between the colour you put in your hair today and the one you had in it this morning which differs from it by one millionth of a shade. We know all your female friends will squeal with delight at this miniscule change but, trust us, we really, honestly don't know – it's the way our brains are wired up.

We cannot read your mind. Unless you tell us what you want we cannot give it to you. Honestly.

You cannot read our minds. You do not know what we 'really' meant. Honestly.

Why absent dads matter

Here we go, dad-bashing again, I thought, when I read a report that the British government is to introduce courses to encourage 'disengaged fathers' to get involved with their children.

Then I came to the bit that said almost half the children from separated families in a UK survey did not see their father last year – a remarkable figure. Suddenly the idea of encouraging 'disengaged fathers' to build relationships with their children did not seem so bad after all.

And when Mary Corcoran of the Department of Sociology at NUI Maynooth sent me a report on research she did on 'absent' fathers in Ireland, it struck me that we need something similar here.

In Ireland, the issue seems to be how to get single young men, especially from low-income areas, to involve themselves with their children. These single young men are probably not reading *The Irish Times,* nor are they writing for it, so why should we care? We should care because the involvement of these young men with their children, now and in the future, can improve the whole quality of life for all of society.

American research shows that the children of 'absent' fathers are less likely to get into trouble with the law if their fathers take an interest in them. In the UK in 2001, a clinical psychologist, Jenny Taylor, interviewed two groups of boys in south London. One group had no criminal convictions and had never caused trouble to their teachers. Of these, 80 per cent said they were close to their fathers. The other group had criminal convictions and were in a secure unit. Of these, almost half could not identify a father figure in their lives. Of the 'good boys', as she called them in her report, just over half lived with their biological father and one-quarter had an absent father who was, nevertheless, involved in their lives. Almost none of the 'bad boys' were living with their father. The involvement of a father – present or absent – who disapproves of anti-social behaviour and whose love and approval the child does not want to jeopardise seems to be the protective factor.

In Ireland, the 'bad boys' wouldn't be in a secure unit in the first place because we don't bother our heads about things like that. Therefore the benefits of encouraging young, single fathers to take an interest in their kids would be even greater in this country, given our 'free range' attitude to problem behaviour.

What Mary Corcoran found was that separated fathers who had previously been married and involved in rearing their children were far more likely to stay involved than single fathers. Indeed, in her report in the *Irish Journal of Sociology*, she remarks that some of these men go to 'extraordinary lengths' to build and maintain contact.

It is the young men who have never been married and never been much involved in the rearing of the child that need encouragement. They have become fathers under what she calls 'spontaneous and contingent circumstances' – the most polite description I have ever heard of casual sex. These young men tend to have neither money nor the emotional maturity to involve themselves in the rearing of their children. Minding the child the odd time – or getting their own parents to do it – buying presents and providing some meagre financial support seems to be as much as they do.

Some of those in her research wanted to make something of their lives because of becoming fathers, but this desire does not always translate into action. Mary Corcoran suggests that if they were encouraged to build a positive involvement with their children, both they and their children would benefit.

The rest of us would benefit too. These may be young men we would cross the road to avoid – but if education and other means can be used to get them involved with their kids, our streets will be safer to walk down in the future.

Happy Christmas? Speak for yourself!

There is no law written down anywhere that obliges you to have a happy Christmas.

I think that is important to say at this time of year. The marketing industry would have us believe that everybody else is going to have a wonderful Christmas because they're buying the right drinks, driving the right cars, wearing the right clothes, eating in the right places and, well, generally doing everything right.

Every man, this myth would have it, has a glamorous girlfriend or wife on whom the snowflakes fall gently under the stars as Santa appears around the corner in his sleigh. There is a blazing log fire inside. The children are all cute and would never dream of calling you, their father, a dork. Of course, it's not true. Moreover, we know it's not true but somehow we contrive to feel aggrieved or even guilty if we are not happy enough at this time of year.

The problem with insisting on being happy at Christmas is that we can inflict extra pain on ourselves and on others when we fail to achieve this ideal. Drinking too much, taking drugs, fighting with people and brooding and moping are all things we do to try to get rid of negative feelings. Very often, though, we would do better to allow ourselves simply to experience the negativity, which, if it is allowed to, will pass. Allowing it to pass means not talking endlessly to yourself about what's going wrong but getting on with whatever it is you need to do today.

Consider the matter of involvement with other people. This is the time of year when most of us have closer contact with colleagues, friends and relatives than at any other. However, we need to be able to accept that not all of this involvement will be pure fun.

For instance, some people simply do not enjoy office parties at which you get to spend ages listening to some very drunk person explaining to you how he would reorganise the purchasing department if only the management had the good sense to put him in charge. Similarly, visits to relatives are not always an unalloyed pleasure around Christmas. Some visits will be boring, others irritating.

Despite the irritations, however, we know that involvement with other people can be life-saving. We need involvement – it's good for our mental and physical health. We are less likely to be depressed and less likely to take our own lives if we have good relationships with others.

But to be with people we have to have the capacity to put up with feeling negative some of the time. We humans are contrary. We can be a bit spiky with other humans. We tend to be motivated more by what we want than by what the other guy wants. So we're not as easy to be with as we would like to imagine. Therefore in order to be with people we need to develop a tolerance of discomfort and annoyance because these are all part of the package.

I think this is especially so around Christmas Day and St Stephen's Day. What seems to happen is that people who can usually tolerate each other good-humouredly for an hour at a time are put into a sort of social pressure cooker and made to stay there for hour after hour. The pressure rises as alcohol is applied. Yet if people can get through the day without the lid blowing off, they are likely to feel a glow of well-being for having been there.

What will blow the lid off is the person who cannot tolerate being irritated or discomfited and who makes sure everybody else gets to know about it.

Now, I would like you, me and everybody else to have a happy Christmas. But if you are going to be unhappy or irritated, at least don't worsen the experience by feeling angry, guilty or aggrieved about the fact.

In short, if you want to be unhappy or fed up go right ahead and be my guest. Bah. Humbug.

How fathers can help the children when mothers are depressed

From a study of the effects of depression in mothers has emerged new evidence of the powerful long-term effects of a father's involvement with his children.

It is a sad fact that chronic depression in a mother leaves children more vulnerable to problems of their own later on – they are at higher risk than other children of becoming depressed themselves, of suffering from anxiety, of behaving aggressively or of being hyperactive. Just why this is so is not clear. Depression makes the mother emotionally absent and perhaps it is that absence that accounts for these effects.

The good news, though, is that the father can greatly reduce these effects by ensuring that he is closely involved with the children.

This may seem obvious, but it's easier said than done. A mother's depression casts a cloud over a family. If a mother is depressed it is easy enough for the father to become a little depressed or upset himself by this and not to have as much time for the children as he would otherwise.

However, if the father is aware of how important his involvement is to his children's long-term future then hopefully he will be able to ensure that they have a parent who is fully emotionally present. What does that mean? The research, conducted at St Louis University, suggests that involvement means such things as listening to what the children have to say, discussing important family decisions with them, attending school concerts and other similar events and knowing where they are when they are not at home.

So we are not talking about something incredibly complicated to understand. This is not nuclear physics. Yet sometimes these are the very things that a man under the stress of trying to make a living and keep the household running might be tempted to ignore. After all, if you are supporting your family and looking after their basic needs while also trying to help your wife in her depression, you may feel that you are more than sufficiently involved.

This sort of involvement is what might be regarded as emotional involvement. Attending a school concert is not just about watching your child perform: it's about the emotional effect of the whole experience for the child and the emotional value to the child of your presence there.

The research was conducted over a number of years with more than 6,500 mothers and children as part of a bigger study. The lead researcher, Jen Jen Chang PhD, had grown up with a depressed sister and had observed how depression had affected the whole family. This got her wondering how a mother's depression would affect the family and what could be done to alleviate the effects. She advocates that health professionals ensure that fathers know the importance of their role in relation to the children's emotional well-being when the mother is depressed.

Her findings back up other studies on the importance to a child's well-being of a father's involvement. For instance, Barnardo's 'Da' project in Ballyfermot has found that fathers' involvement means better social skills for the children, fewer emotional and behavioural difficulties in adolescence, better school performance and less chance of getting into trouble with the law.

Some people already know this instinctively – but others do not realise how very important their emotional involvement is to their children. Fathers were for too long encouraged by society to see themselves as breadwinners alone and perhaps, additionally, as authority figures, but not necessarily to see the importance of emotional involvement with their children.

Men who are low in self-esteem or in self-confidence, who perhaps have never been told very many positive things about themselves, may not realise how important they are to their children.

So if we want to boost the future of our children we need to begin by telling fathers just how much they matter. And we shouldn't assume that they already know.

Men fighting domestic violence

Some years ago I met a group of people with physical disabilities and, in the course of conversation, I asked if all of them had been born with their disabilities. All had except one: a woman who had been so badly beaten by her husband that he had left her disabled for life and unable, ever again, to live independently.

I thought of her when I read, in a new report from the Women's Health Council (www.whc.ie), that in Europe more women die or are seriously injured every year through domestic violence than through cancer or road accidents. The report acknowledges that men suffer violence at the hands of women – but all the evidence, I'm afraid, suggests that men carry out most of the violence that occurs between the genders.

What's going on with men who are violent towards their female partners? A few, I suspect, don't know any better. It's what they grew up with. Most people who see violence at home avoid repeating it in their own relationships later on. Some, however, think it's the thing to do.

Others, though, seem to have a pathological need to control their partners. Everything – what she wears, who she sees, how much make-up she puts on, who she talks to at work, who she telephones, when and how she does housework – has to be controlled in detail.

I suspect that behind this pathological need for control is a dread of losing the other person, a certainty that she will leave unless she is put on the very tightest of reins. The irony, of course, is that these control freaks generally end up losing their partners anyhow – by holding on to them so oppressively they drive them away.

Women who are violent and abusive to their male partners may have similar motivations. A new book, *That Bitch: Protect Yourself Against Women with Malicious Intent* (www.thatbitchbook.com), written by Mary T. Cleary, founder of Amen, and journalist Roy Sheppard, describes instance after instance of such behaviour. I don't like the title, which was chosen to shock, because I think it creates an unnecessary barrier between men and women on this issue. That said, the book does a good job of highlighting one big problem concerning violence by women towards men. This is the reluctance of men to speak out because they have a realistic fear of not being believed or of being sneered at.

An interesting campaign to bring together both of these aspects of domestic violence – men as perpetrators and men as victims – has been launched in the UK. The No Slap, Just Tickle campaign (www.noslapjusttickle.com) aims to help men speak out against, and overcome, domestic violence, whether they are victims, perpetrators or bystanders.

The inclusion of perpetrators may seem odd but many violent men go through periods of remorse and this is something that can be built on by a campaign like this. The campaign urges men who perpetrate violence to have the courage to seek help and to understand that domestic violence is never acceptable. There are programmes to help such men run by MOVE Ireland (www.moveireland.ie) in ten locations around the country and contact numbers are given on the website.

The No Slap, Just Tickle campaign encourages men who are victims of domestic violence to 'have the courage to seek help – even if you have the impression that it will make matters worse. As a man you are no different to the countless women who have spoken out about domestic violence and freed themselves from it'. Amen (www.amen.ie) can be a helpful resource to men in this situation. The campaign encourages men who are aware of situations of domestic violence to 'urge the person in question to seek help – whether as a victim or as a perpetrator'.

Domestic violence is a choice. The men and women who perpetrate it do not, for example, have uncontrollable urges to beat up their bosses at work. Therefore if they beat up or torment one person and not another they are exercising a choice. That is a fact we need to bear in mind at all times.

Domestic violence is surrounded by choices. The violent partner, who must carry the moral as well as the legal responsibility for his or her acts, can choose to seek help. So can the person who is the target of domestic violence. Opening your mind to the possibility of choice is the first step towards ending this wretched situation.

Getting dumped

I once got dumped by a girlfriend at a John O'Connor recital in the Pro-Cathedral in Dublin.

I always thought it a pretty classy way to be given the push. She proved her credentials as a music lover by waiting for the last concert in the series before turning to me during a lull in the performance and whispering, 'I think we ought to stop seeing each other'.

Actually, I seem to have had a history of classy brush-offs. Another lady signalled the end of our relationship by informing me, as she stepped into a taxi, that she would be spending the next week on a yacht with a man she had met recently. Actually, she continued, she had been sailing with this chap last weekend when she was supposed to be staying with her mother. You have to appreciate that back in the Dark Ages only a small minority of very rich people had yachts – so as I trudged off into the night I had the small consolation of knowing I had been in touch, however vicariously, with the world of wealth.

I also got dropped by letter, which I suppose is sophisticated compared to the text message and the e-mail. Back then, people knew about grammar, syntax and where to stick their apostrophes so at least you were terminated with some degree of elegance when it was done via the postman. I myself dumped somebody by letter once, a fact of which I am not proud.

Still, it can be worse. Consider the experience of the guy whose ex-wife gleefully told the *Sydney Morning Herald's MashUp* blog how she did the deed. She took her husband's laptop, PlayStation, favourite clothes and other cherished items and threw them into his brand new Porsche. Then she drove the car away and abandoned it in a dodgy public place with the doors open and the keys still in the ignition. Before getting into the taxi that brought her away from there, she took a picture of the car with her camera phone. In a touch of inspired, vindictive genius, she did not send the photograph to her husband until the following morning. By the time he found the car, it had been stolen, burgled, driven at high speed and set on fire. Her excuse for this regrettable behaviour, by the way, was that she had caught him in bed with her cousin.

Most of us, when we get dumped, just go off and lick our wounds or make an appointment to see a solicitor. But some manage to get a thrill out of it that lasts for years. I knew a woman who was told by her fiancé as they walked along a beach on a moonlit night that he had met somebody else and would not be marrying her after all. In a sort of calm fury she slowly removed the engagement ring, which had cost him thousands and thousands, and flung it into the sea. Years later, she still got a kick out of his look of anguish as he watched all that money disappear into the Mediterranean.

Today, technology offers ways of dumping your lover that make writing a letter look like an exercise in courtesy. Nowadays many get the news via a text message that says 'It's over', without the apostrophe, of course. You can even go to a website called dearjohn.com that will generate a break-up letter for you that you can then e-mail to the one who is no longer the love of your life. It gives you the option of blaming yourself or the dumpee, of being kind or cruel.

Bad? Probably even worse is the method recommended on another blog: borrow a baby and, while changing its nappy in front of your horrified soon-to-be ex-lover, apologise for never having mentioned it before and explain that its other parent has abandoned said baby to your care. But the wonderful thing is, you add, 'I am not alone. I have you now and together we can rear this wonderful baby as our own.' Works every time.

I just love your body fat!

Is your ideal partner, the one you fantasise about spending the rest of your life with, as slim as a greyhound? If so, the bad news is that if you want to attract this gorgeous skinny creature, you're going to have to get skinny yourself.

People get together for reasons that are not apparent to them at the time and the most recently discovered source of mutual attraction turns out to be body fat. A study of forty-two couples in Aberdeen found that people tend to be attracted to others who have the same amount of fat on them. So if you are thin, you are likely to 'end up' – if that's not too pessimistic a phrase to use about marriage – with somebody who's thin. If you're plump, you are likely to walk up the aisle with another plump person.

The researchers who did this study point out that it wasn't always like that. Back when people used to get married in their early twenties, it was still too early for either to know if the other would put on weight. Nowadays we put off marriage and having children to a much later time, which gives us the opportunity to add on the pounds. Therefore we are now more likely to know who's our match when it comes to body mass.

This probably all has something to do with conformity. We like to think that we are mad romantics who will follow love wherever we find it, but it's not like that. However non-conformist we may believe ourselves to be, we will almost certainly marry into our own social class and our spouse will have a broadly equivalent income. So it is not all that surprising that we are also attracted to people who are similar to us in terms of weight.

Some commentators have unkindly suggested that this could contribute to the increase in obesity as large persons marry each other and give birth to children who are genetically disposed to piling on the weight. That sounds a bit alarmist to me. However, I have seen the theory about like attracting like borne out at a holiday apartment where the food was 'free' in the sense that you didn't have to pay anything extra for what you ate during your stay. There I saw entire families of incredibly large people eating all they could get. Sometimes you saw an obese person with a thinnish person but more often everybody in the family was obese and they seemed to float as they carefully balanced their overloaded trays between serving counter and table.

What this research suggests is that the couples in these families didn't get obese because they were married and comfortable. They got married because they were obese. Does that mean they have no incentive to change? One of the more interesting findings in research on couples is that if one of them decides to behave in a more healthy way then there is a good chance the other will do the same.

In our more cynical moments we might complain that our spouses have driven us to drink, but the research shows that our spouse may very well drive us off the drink by cutting down or giving it up herself. This copycat effect is particularly strong for drinking and smoking. We influence each other more than we think.

And what this means, of course, is that if you want your spouse to behave in a more healthy way – by losing weight for example – your best chance of getting her to do so is to adopt a healthy diet yourself. So we're back to where we started: be the way you want the other person to be.

Meanwhile, if you're single, do you want a glimpse of the future? Want to know what your spouse will look like? Spend a little time in front of the mirror. She'll look a lot like what you see there.

Coming to terms with being gay – not so easy

I wonder how many gay men cringe when they see camp depictions of gayness on Coronation Street or on some of Graham Norton's shows?

I am not suggesting that these depictions are invalid or, heaven forbid, that Graham Norton is not real. However, it seems to me that the camp image of gay people has hijacked reality. Camp gay people there certainly are, and that's fine. But if campness is depicted by the media as the predominant expression of gayness, then where does that leave the majority of gay people who are not camp and who do not want to be seen as camp?

For instance, I can only imagine the distress felt by a young teenager who has realised that he is gay but who would find it agonisingly embarrassing to be regarded as one of those exotic people camping it up on television.

Teenagers are a paradox. On the one hand, they are going through the process of separating psychologically from their parents and would be the first to tell you they don't care a fig (or something else starting with an 'f') for conformity. On the other hand, they have a desperate need to conform to their peer group.

Given that gay people form a minority of the population, it follows that the other members of the peer group of the average gay teenager are probably not gay. What would be the result of coming out to that group? I suspect that in almost all cases the response would be acceptance and perhaps, even, 'So what?' And yet the thought of coming out to one's friends must be frightening, especially since their views of gayness are likely to have been shaped by depictions of very camp people on television.

This, I suspect, is more of a problem for gay male teenagers than for gay female teenagers. The media likes to depict gay females as looking, sounding and acting the same as any other females. In other words it sticks closer to reality when depicting gay females.

Acceptance from one's own peer group is one thing but teenagers tend to be very scathing about persons who are not members of their group. So coming out to your own peer group may not be so bad – it may be the reactions of people from outside the group that worry a gay teenager.

For these reasons I was delighted to read that groups for gay and lesbian young people are to be established around the country with the help of the HSE and the Departments of Education and Community, Rural and Gaeltacht Affairs. This work is being spearheaded by a Dublin-based group called Belong To that helps gay young people between fourteen and twenty-three years of age to meet in a safe and relaxed environment.

Michael Barron, the group's national coordinator, recently told *The Irish Times* that the number of young people coming to the project's groups in Dublin has been more than doubling each year. Some people travel to the groups from various parts of the country every week.

Mr Barron also pointed out that young people are increasingly willing to come out to their families and friends. However, I see that a survey of its readers by *Gay Community News* found that while 80 per cent of respondents are 'out' to their friends, only 60 per cent are out to their family and only 50 per cent to everyone at their workplace.

But there must also be many people who wouldn't know where to get *Gay Community News*, who certainly wouldn't march into a newsagent in their local town and order it and who would not want to be seen reading it. Among that group the level of concealment, and consequently of social isolation, must be high.

So the work done by Belong To is of enormous importance. But I am afraid that for as long as we in the media continue to equate gay males with Graham Norton stereotypes many young men will continue to choose social isolation.

There is more information on Belong To at http://www.gayswitchboard.ie/outyouth.htm and the group can be contacted at belongto@eircom.net or 0–18734184.

Men in cardigans – a stitch too far?

Has the man who puts on a cardigan passed a momentous milestone in his life? Is he indicating that he is no longer for the wars and that, so to speak, 'home is the sailor from the sea, the hunter from the hill'? Is it time for a good snooze, a mug of hot chocolate and early to bed? Or is he making an up-to-the-minute fashion statement?

To me, the wearing of a cardigan is something I would have to psychologically and emotionally adjust to in the same way that I would have to adjust to the use of, say, a Zimmer frame. I would have to say goodbye to that part of my old identity that had no connection whatsoever with the cardigan and all that it implies.

To my mind the cardigan implies pipe, slippers and your faithful old dog dozing at your feet as you peruse the obituary columns, chortling occasionally to your wife – who is arranging flowers in a vase – at the demise of some old enemy.

The thing is, I could be wrong about all this. In the UK, sales of cardigans have increased tenfold in some leading retailers in the past year. Even David Beckham has taken to wearing a cardigan occasionally. There again, David Beckham has been known to wear his wife's hairband, her knickers and a sari, so perhaps he is not the most reliable guide to what's coming next for today's man.

I learnt all this from listening to an item on *Woman's Hour* on BBC Radio Four. And, yes, I fully realise that this means I should probably be wearing a cardigan myself. But I have resisted and I hope to continue to resist any involvement with this garment.

Who could be buying all these cardigans in the UK? Surely not the big lad with the blade-one haircut, the T-shirt stretched over the belly and the dozen cans of Dutch Gold in the plastic bag? I think we can safely say that in such an eventuality, John Bull's image would become rather less frightening to the rest of us.

The cardigan does, though, have a link with war. The interknit, sorry, internet informs me that it is named for the seventh Earl of Cardigan and the knitted vest he wore before leading his men to their deaths in the Charge of the Light Brigade. One wonders whether any of these unfortunates questioned the wisdom of going into battle led by a man wearing a cardigan? There again, the ill-fated charge is said to have resulted from a bungled communication from the British commander Lord Raglan, another chap with the same name as a knitted garment. And, of course, the whole sorry affair occurred in a place called Balaclava. I think we are beginning to get a pattern here, and it's a knitting pattern.

If that's not enough to deter today's man from taking up the wearing of cardigans, then I suppose we must expect matters to get even worse. Will we see a return of the leather patch at the elbow of your tweed jacket? Be warned – the wearing of such patches involves adopting a serious look as though you are so busy studying the Greek and Latin masters that you haven't the time to kit yourself out in decent clothes. The ultimate degradation would be socks with sandals and, on very hot days on the beach, a white handkerchief on your head with each corner knotted for ballast.

What are the health implications of the cardigan? I suppose you could argue that the cardigan wearer could reduce his stress levels by fiddling with his buttons, like worry beads. And I don't suppose the cardigan wearer will want to go boy racing, taking drugs (except those prescribed by his doctor) or drinking cider at midnight on the canal bank. All that is to the good. But is it enough to justify the risk of hurtling down the slippery slope towards socks with sandals and handkerchiefs on heads?

I think not.

Forever young and irritating

Are you by any chance, a kidult? A kidult is an adult who has never really grown up and who is in no hurry to do so. Generally speaking, kidults are in no hurry to grow up because they're having too much fun or they are scared of taking on responsibility, or both.

The kidult has been around for ages. I remember Gay Byrne reading out letters on his radio programme from mothers fed up with sons who refused to grow up but preferred to lie around being fed and watered by their parents. These letters tended to elicit an outraged response from the 'Give him a good kick up the arse' brigade.

I wonder what happened to these kidults? Did they run into strong women who took them in hand and made men of them? Did some of them find wives who took up where mother left off? Perhaps some are still sprawled on the sofa preparing to apply for the pension as mother, now in her eighties, keeps them in beer, cigarettes and pizzas.

Today's kidult, as I understand the concept, does more than lie on the sofa. Do you, perhaps, put on short trousers and a baseball cap, worn backwards, at the weekends and go skateboarding around the streets of our great cities? If so, you may be a kidult and that may be the kindest thing you've been called in a long time.

If you're in your thirties, forties or fifties and you go out on the pull (you are not, of course, married), do you ignore women of your own age and head straight for girls in their twenties? If so, you are definitely a kidult. Do you spend hours with your PlayStation 3? Kidult again.

Perhaps you even jet off to London now and then, kit yourself out in a school uniform and dance, drink and snog the night away at the school disco scene? (Let me say straight away, in case there is any confusion about this, that I only know about the school disco scene because I looked it up on Wikipedia. It's a long time since I've been in short pants.)

I may have given the impression here that the kidults of the past were exclusively slobs who lounged around on sofas in their parents' living rooms. This is not an entirely complete picture. Many of you may not know that there was a time when there was no such thing as an ATM machine. So if you ran out of cash in the evening or at the weekend you were in trouble, especially if you were a kidult looking to impress the girls. One kidult I knew solved this problem and enhanced his status by opening a bank account in the Dublin Airport branch of the Bank of Ireland that was open outside normal hours. If he ran out of money at the weekend he would simply nip out to the airport in his snippy, jazzy car and make a withdrawal. This sort of thing was just perfect for impressing the sort of girls who were impressed by this sort of thing.

There are, let it be said, female kidults too. You are still a student in your thirties? If so, you may well be a female kidult, a sort of eternal schoolgirl who doesn't have to face the world for as long as Daddy keeps paying the bills. Does Daddy still pay for your health insurance? Does he take your car for its NCT test? All these may be symptoms of the female kidult. Here's another sign: has your boyfriend put you on his credit card? If so, you are probably a kidult and he is probably an eejit. Don't let him get away.

The phenomenon of the kidult goes back even further than the time of Gay Byrne. Bachelors were taxed in ancient Rome. And early in the last century, the Italian government imposed a tax on bachelors unless they had joined a religious order and taken a vow of chastity.

Now there's an idea for the next kidult you spot skateboarding around the IFSC.

The Irish mammy as endangered species

Is the Irish mammy in danger of being driven into oblivion by the yummy mummy? And would it be an entirely bad thing if she was?

The Irish mammy, as we know, adores her golden boy. No other woman can ever live up to her devotion to her son and this is made clear to any woman who has the temerity to become his wife.

Sometimes sonny boy continues to visit his mammy for his dinner on a daily basis as his wife sits at home and grinds her teeth. Years ago, Gay Byrne read out a letter on his radio show from a wife complaining that her husband's mammy still made guggie for him every day. Guggie is made by boiling an egg, chopping it up in a cup and mixing it with butter while still hot. It's very tasty and it's something I have not had since I was a child because, generally speaking, it is something you would only make for a child. Anyway, it appears that this particular golden boy was very attached to his guggie, which is not the sort of thing your wife will usually make for you. So mammy had to step into the breach.

That, I think you will agree, was a true Irish mammy. Perhaps she has passed on by now. If so, I wonder has the wife relented and begun to make guggie for him every day or is it a case of 'You just can't make guggie like my mammy used to do?'

Irish mammies and their favourite sons constitute a mutual admiration society, according to Irish blogger Paige Harrison who writes the *blankpaige* blog. The world has heard of the Irish mammy, she suggests, 'partly because their sons wax lyrical about their incomparable brilliance'. Paige thinks there is scope for evening things out a bit in favour of the Irish daddy. 'Maybe it's time that Irish daughters did the same for their fathers and transformed the daddy into a role that young men would be proud of,' she writes in a comment on my blog.[1]

She was responding to an item about a scheme in Leeds in which young fathers are taught basic childcare skills. These young men, many of whom are not living with the mothers of their children, learn to prepare baby food, change nappies, bring their babies to the park and so on. The coordinators of the scheme, called Fathers and Children Together, say most of the skills taught to these young fathers have been requested by themselves.

You can imagine how a genuine Irish mammy would respond to all of this. A young man being taught to change nappies and prepare baby food while there is a mother there who is perfectly capable of doing all these things? Can't you just hear generations of Irish mammies spinning in their graves?

Yes, graves, because I wonder if the Irish mammy is becoming a thing of the past. Can you see today's yummy mummy, flying around the place in her SUV and nibbling a carrot for lunch, can you really see her dragging herself out of the gym to make a nice cup of guggie for her son before he goes home to his inadequate wife?

I think not. The Irish mammy has fallen victim to an increasingly self-centred and materialistic society in which women expect to be able to give up minding their sons after they get married.

Perhaps it is all for the best, though. You will not see a yummy mummy producing a cholesterol-drenched full Irish breakfast for her darling boy. Nor will you see her insisting that he sit down on the sofa and have a nice rest – when he could be out having a healthy jog.

And the result of the yummy mummy's fixation with diet and fitness? Why it's that golden boy will be only too keen to run home to his missus for some real mollycoddling. And who knows, she might even whip him up a nice helping of guggie.

1. www.justlikeaman.blogspot.com.

Mr Peg and other euphemisms

Good morning. And how is Mr Peg today? And Percy and Moose and Maggot and Mr Happy? These, if you haven't guessed, are names of men's penises, as given to them by the men themselves or by their adoring partners.

They are among the names that emerged in a survey by Male Health, an excellent and lively men's health website (www.malehealth.co.uk). Other names include Dick, Willy, Charlie, Herbie, Trevor, Big Ben, Percy the Small Engine, Rodney, Junior and Wild Thing.

Notice that there are no specifically Irish names in there. Not a single Tadhg, Séamus or Ciarán, for instance. Perhaps, given his apparent alacrity in standing up for himself, the nickname, 'a Willie O'Dea', might be adopted for the Irish male member? 'Would you like to come outside and meet Willie O'Dea?' could become a preamble to all sorts of excitement, which, of course, might later have to be denied.

Anyway, penises are a serious matter and if you've been reading your spam emails lately, you'll know that one of the most widespread concerns men have about Mr Peg is his size. This, as it happens, is something that worries men a lot more than it worries women.

A recent issue of *BJU International* looked at the findings of studies on penises since 1942. This is the sort of heroic thing that the world's researchers do and for which I hope they are appropriately rewarded. *BJU International* is a journal that provides bedtime reading for the world's urologists, so this is serious stuff. Its editor-in-chief, by the way, is an Irishman, Professor John Fitzpatrick of UCD.

Anyway, the researchers found that 85 per cent of women say they are satisfied with the size of their partner's penis. However, only 55 per cent of men are satisfied with the size of their own members. In fact, for women the man's personality is a great deal more important than the size of Big Ben. All of which must be a great disappointment for men who go to the expense of having cosmetic surgery to increase their penis size but who neglect to do any work on their own personalities.

It appears that about two-thirds of men who are worried about penis size can trace their anxieties back to comparisons made in childhood. Over one-third develop worries after observing the size of other men's members in pornography. It appears to have passed them by that the men in pornographic films and pictures are probably chosen partly because of having a penis size which is larger than average. As well as surgery, men try to increase penis size through things such as diet, ointments, vacuum pumps and even sticking poor Mr Peg into a concoction of salt and cold tea.

Doctors who study this sort of thing say men are generally poor at comparing their own penis size with that of other men. This is because the man sees his own penis from above and this perspective makes the size seem smaller than it really is. So small penis size may be a visual illusion – but it's an illusion that will continue to make money for the spammers for as long as the World Wide Web exists.

You can read more on the BJU research report on www.malehealth.co.uk, a website that is worth visiting from time to time anyhow.

And if you want to find out more about penises in general, you could book a trip to Iceland and visit the Icelandic Phallological Museum, which describes itself as 'probably the only museum in the world to contain a collection of phallic specimens belonging to all the various types of mammal found in a single country'. I love that – 'probably'. No, guys, you're the only one. It is reported that they have been promised a human penis to make their collection complete.

Anyway they have a rather dull website – www.phallus.is – which you navigate through by clicking on a penis. But don't let the boss catch you at it. That would be worse than getting Mr Peg caught in your zip.

Platonic relationships – passion without sex

Platonic relationships are little talked about today. Whether they are between men and women, women and women, or men and men they are likely to be seen as a sort of cover for a sexual relationship.

For many centuries, the non-sexual platonic relationship was quite accepted. But in the twentieth century, a growing scepticism about the possibility of passionate affection without sex has made such relationships unfashionable.

When the BBC's *Woman's Hour* recently broadcast two programmes on platonic relationships, the programme makers appeared to regard these as relationships in which one or the other partner either would not or could not have sex, though the other person in the equation still wanted it. Sometimes the decision not to have sex was made by the man, sometimes by the woman. Their partners said they missed the affection that went with sex.

In a sense the programmes were misnamed. A platonic relationship in the sense derived from philosophers such as Plato and Socrates involves a deep feeling, even a passion for the other person. It is non-sexual but the passion is there nevertheless.

When the American poet Emily Dickinson wrote to her friend Sue Gilbert in the nineteenth century, 'If you were here – and Oh that you were, my Susie, we need not talk at all, our eyes would whisper for us, and your hand fast in mine we would not ask for language ... I try to bring you nearer ...', she was expressing a platonic relationship. There is no reason to believe there was any sexual wish involved.

And when, three centuries earlier, Shakespeare wrote to his 'Fair Lord' in one of 126 sonnets addressed to him,

Shall I compare thee to a summer's day?
Thou art more lovely and more temperate.

this was not taken at the time to refer to homosexual love in the sexual sense.

So what is the state of the platonic relationship today? I have no doubt that such relationships are more likely to be found between men and women than between men and men or between women and women.

If your same-sex friend was to tell you, in the equivalent twenty-first century language, that 'we need not talk at all, our eyes will whisper for us' or, 'thou art more lovely and temperate than a summer's day', you would be likely to assume that this person fancied you and wanted to get you into their bed. And that assumption, in most cases, would wreck the relationship.

For men and women to have a non-sexual, deep relationship on the other hand is not all that uncommon. When two friends in the UK, Susie King and her friend Jeanne, set up a website called platonicpartners.co.uk they found that half the people who joined up were men. The website describes itself as 'celebrating celibate, platonic, non-physical or partly physical relationships, where you can meet other like-minded people, explore a holistic, integrated lifestyle and get ideas of where to look for support'.

Susie told *Woman's Hour* that what people most miss in a sex-free relationship is the affection linked with sex, the cuddles and intimacy. I think this again is a new, twenty-first century definition of the platonic friendship. In the old definition deep affection, though it might not be physical, would have been regarded as something without which the platonic relationship simply would not exist.

People who have seen sex leave their relationships for medical reasons also miss the physical affection, yet there is no particular reason why that level of affection should not continue. Again, it is a peculiarly twentieth and twenty-first century idea that physical affection is necessarily a prelude to sex.

If the concept of the platonic relationship has lasted so long I think it is because it meets a need in humans for a close relationship with another that doesn't necessarily have to include sex.

So the next time you hear people sniggering about somebody having a platonic relationship with somebody else, remember that it might just be a more genuine and deep relationship than any currently experienced by the people doing the sniggering.

The hidden crime of male rape

Male rape is a hidden crime of our time. Rape crisis centres increasingly hear about male rape but few cases ever come to trial. Yet the Dublin Rape Crisis Centre says 12 per cent of its clients are male and that it expects this proportion to grow.

The phenomenon of male rape is concealed mainly by the reluctance of its victims to come forward. Heterosexual men may fear that they will be accused of being gay. Gay men may fear that they will be seen to have put themselves into circumstances in which rape could take place. In other words, they fear what has often prevented female rape victims from coming forward, namely that they will be accused of having asked for it.

Indeed, the tendency to blame rape victims for what has been done to them has been well established in research. Therefore, one can see that a man who is raped might be more reluctant, for this reason, to come forward.

Matters are complicated where the man has experienced a physiological response of arousal to whatever acts were performed. Indeed, some rapists aim to bring about such a response as part of the abuse of the victim and to deter him from going to the police. The response, if it occurs, is no more than a mechanical one, so to speak, and it in no way mitigates the enormity of the crime that has been committed. Nevertheless, the victim may feel shame and embarrassment and therefore be reluctant to reveal what happened.

Male rape is carried out by both heterosexual and homosexual men. Indeed, there is reason to suspect that most male rapes are carried out by heterosexual men. This is understandable when you realise that rape has less to do with physical attraction than with power, control and rage. Therefore it is not necessary to be in a gay 'setting' or environment for a rape to happen – it can happen anywhere and to anyone. And it is more likely that the man will know his attacker in some way than that the perpetrator will be a complete stranger.

Yet the rape is traumatic and help is needed. For instance, research into this phenomenon would suggest that a man who is raped is more likely than a woman to be gang-raped. There is also a real possibility that he will be physically assaulted in other ways as well.

We read and hear about horrific physical attacks on women who are raped. These attacks amplify the effect of the rape itself. The same is true of male rape victims.

Traditionally, we think of prison as a place in which men can be sexually abused and raped by other men. I have never heard of cases of rape in Irish prisons. But we know, from research and investigations, about the rape of men by men in US and Australian prisons. This is often jokingly referred to in American movies in a way that would never happen in relation to the rape of women.

Do we believe that Irish prisoners are somehow inherently more decent than US or Australian prisoners? I don't, and I suspect that sexual abuse and harassment of men in the prisons is also a problem in this country, but one we never hear about, possibly due to a combination of shame and fear.

Men who have been raped can and do recover but this is more likely to happen and to happen more quickly if they get help. Dublin Rape Crisis Centre is at 1800 778 888 and its email address is rcc@indigo.ie. There are almost twenty rape crisis centres outside Dublin and you can find information on them by going to the website of Dublin Rape Crisis Centre at www.drcc.ie and clicking on the 'Contact us' link.

If you have been raped or sexually assaulted but you are not yet ready to seek direct help, at least read the material for male survivors of rape at www.secasa.com.au, an excellent Australian website. Click the 'Survivors' link on the front page to get to the material for men.

The pain of shyness

I was much shyer when I was in my late teens than I am today and one of the great discoveries of my life was that other people didn't know what I was going through. I found this out when a colleague casually remarked that I was 'as cool as a cucumber'. In reality, I was experiencing agonies of shyness but the discovery that other people interpreted this as confidence helped me to take the risk of social involvement.

And shyness is, indeed, an agony when at its most intense. I suspect that the agony is greater for men than for women. This is because even in the twenty-first century it is the men who are expected to approach the women for dates and dances. Indeed, you don't have to be shy to have experienced the 'will she, won't she, will I make a fool of myself?' drama that can go on in the head of a man trying to pluck up the courage to ask a woman for a date. If anything, the business of asking for a dance is worse – that walk across the floor can seem as long and as daunting as a journey to the Antarctic.

There are certain errors that shy people make and which worsen this wretched condition. First, they assume that other people can see how shy they are. That is why it can be liberating to realise that this is not so, as I mentioned at the start of this piece.

The second error is to assume that other people are thinking about you to the exclusion of almost anything else. A shy person will walk past a bus queue and assume that they are being scrutinised by everybody standing there. In reality, the others are almost certainly preoccupied with themselves and some of them wouldn't notice if you stood on your head. Similarly, shy people at a party assume that everybody in the room is looking at them and judging them – a horrible feeling – when nothing of the sort is going on.

Third, shy people tend to compare themselves to the most outgoing person in the room. They could make life easier for themselves by aiming to be average – instead they curl up in a ball because they know they can't measure up to the biggest party animal in the place.

This tendency to demand more of themselves than is reasonable is a major source of pain to shy people. Worse, they tend to assume that other people expect perfection from them when in fact other people, with the exception of a few bullies, are more tolerant and easygoing than the shy person can imagine.

Paradoxically, the shy person is the star in their own drama. That can be said of any of us, but the shy person takes it to an extreme. To the shy person, nobody on the street, in the nightclub or at the party has eyes for anyone else. The shy person, therefore, imagines themselves to be under intense examination at all times.

This can begin to change if the shy person somehow manages to get involved with other people or allows other people to drag them along. Of course, it will still all be agony at first but gradually the shy person's comfort zone will expand. Maybe the shy ones won't ever be the life and soul of the party – though some people hide their shyness behind a façade of confidence – but at least they can be at the party and can function socially with a few people at a time.

If you know somebody who is shy, there is no point in berating them for failing to fight this socially crippling illness. Such criticism will simply drive them further into isolation. It is far better to involve them in things and to accept that they will be the quiet ones in the crowd. This will help them to begin to accept themselves, and acceptance of how they are is perhaps the most important first step on the road out of isolation.

The slave trade still alive in Europe

Two hundred years after the abolition of the transatlantic slave trade, has slavery reached our shores with men as its final customers?

The question is prompted by the announcement that Scotland Yard has set up a unit to combat sex slavery in Britain, just half an hour's flight away. Sex slavery has become a dark aspect of life in Western Europe following the collapse of the old Soviet Union and the Communist regimes of Eastern Europe.

What has that to do with us, you may ask? And what has it to do with the emotional or physical health of men? What it has to do with us is that it is highly unlikely that we have remained untainted by sex slavery. In Britain it is believed that about four thousand women and girls are working as sex slaves. Most have been trafficked into the UK from Eastern Europe, duped into believing that they have been recruited for normal jobs. Some will have been raped and brutalised on the way in order to break their spirit.

Do you believe, or does anyone believe, that nobody has been trafficked onwards into Ireland?

Sex slaves work in brothels and massage parlours paying off a 'debt' arbitrarily set by those who control them. Needless to say, the day never comes when the debt is paid off. We could argue about whether brothels and massage parlours should be licensed and regulated in the interests of the women who work in them. That's another story. Reports suggest that even in Amsterdam with its ultraliberal attitude to sex and its licensed brothels, there is a sort of lower class of sex slaves trafficked from Eastern Europe who work outside the licensed system.

The customers of the sex industry are almost exclusively men. We surely cannot say that there is anything healthy in any sense of the word about having terrified and enslaved women 'servicing' men in these places.

If you included these women as part of society then you would have to say that society is morally damaged by this trade. I would have thought this was true regardless of one's beliefs concerning women who choose to go into the sex industry.

Those who have been enslaved have been trapped by nothing more or less than poverty and by a desire to better their lives. The collapse of industry and of the control exercised over populations by the old Communist regimes has left many young girls growing up to poverty and to very poor prospects indeed. Western Europe is the land of opportunity that draws them from the fields, villages and towns of Eastern Europe. Too often, they are very easy prey for the traffickers. Those involved in trafficking include some women who are in a position to gain the trust of their prospective victims. Taken across the border or to another country, they are sometimes forced into prostitution on the very first day of their arrival.

Police say that women trafficked into the UK and then 'sold' for a few thousand pounds may have to see as many as thirty men a day. And yet the only thing that brought them into these terrible situations was that they were poor and gullible. No doubt many of them had never had sex before in their lives.

The effect on these women must be absolutely devastating. We are all aware of the devastating effects of rape on the lives of its victims. These women are raped every day and many times a day with little or no prospect of escape. It is probably fair to say that the person trafficked out of their home country dies very, very quickly to be replaced by a traumatised shell.

Let's hope our government will play a full part in efforts by the Council of Europe and others to combat this evil trade. For that to happen, however, Irish people need to be aware of sex slavery and to be determined that something should be done about it.

Charles Atlas, from weakling to world's best-developed man

Maybe I read the wrong magazines but the days of the Charles Atlas ads promising that 'you too can have a body like mine' seem to be over.

Now, I do not want a visit from the heirs of 'the World's Most Perfectly Developed Man', as he called himself, so I had better say right now that the Charles Atlas company is alive and well on the Internet.

Throughout much of the twentieth century, Charles Atlas promised that if you bought and faithfully followed his mail-order course you would no longer have to suffer the ignominy of being 'a 97-pound weakling'. Instead, you could develop yourself into a muscular man able to defend his honour and that of his adoring girlfriend.

This really only matters because the Charles Atlas ads provided many young men with an image of how they ought to look. To look like a 97-pound weakling was bad. What happened to such persons was that when they were lying on the beach with their girlfriends they got sand kicked in their eyes by some muscular thug. The only road to redemption was to buy the Charles Atlas course, become a perfectly developed man and take revenge during a future visit to the beach. This redeemed the former weakling in the eyes of his girlfriend.

When I was growing up in Kildare the chances of getting sand kicked in your eyes were remote, unless you happened to be lying in a sandpit at the time and that was a pretty remote possibility too. Indeed, most 97-pound weaklings at the time probably didn't have the price of the course if they lived in Ireland. And even if you could afford it, that meant buying a postal order and the person behind the counter would know exactly what you are doing since everybody had heard of Charles Atlas. This could lead to embarrassing conversations, as it was not an era in which people kept their observations to themselves.

So those of us who saw ourselves as weaklings had to suffer in silence. Is that, I wonder, the reason why I have never had any interest in lying on a beach?

It is said that Charles Atlas himself, originally named Angelo Charles Siciliano, so you can work out where he came from, was himself a weakling who got sand kicked in his eyes by a bully. He responded by becoming a muscle man. In the 1920s he won the title of the World's Most Perfectly Developed Man twice in a row and it was decided that there was really no point in holding it a third time because he would just win it again.

Statues in the US and elsewhere of other great men actually depict Charles Atlas – sometimes from below the neck – because the perfection of his physique brought in commissions to pose for sculptors. He posed for the statue of George Washington in Washington Square Park in New York City.

Although the Charles Atlas physique was marketed as a means of impressing your girlfriend, I suspect it had more to do with impressing other men in the same way that women dress to impress other women, on the basis that men wouldn't really notice if they were wearing a sack.

In Ireland, when Charles Atlas was in his heyday, men were less concerned with their body image than they are now. Today the concern with body image is growing. There are gyms and we can afford to go to them, though I have passed on this option myself and wish I could get back to being a 97-pound weakling.

Becoming a one-man self-admiration society in the gym is one thing. More worryingly, increasing numbers of young men take steroids to build up their muscle mass. In doing so they increase their chances of developing heart disease later on, of developing a psychological dependency and of suffering depression when withdrawing from them.

Frankly, I would rather get sand kicked in my face.

Sex changes widely accepted but not everywhere

When Lib Dem Jenny Bailey became Mayor of Cambridge earlier this year, the UK media sat up and took notice.

Media interest was spurred by the fact that Ms Bailey had been born a man but had a sex change operation about fifteen years ago. Moreover, the Mayoress – traditionally the Mayor's wife – would be Jennifer Liddle, her partner, who was also born as a man and who also had a sex change operation. However, though the media took an interest in this development, it was a fairly mild interest. A few articles appeared and that was that.

All of which indicates acceptance nowadays of the use of surgery to change gender – and that this is no longer seen as a barrier to high political office at local level underlines that acceptance.

Ms Bailey's two sons, aged eighteen and twenty, live with her and her partner. When the media contacted Ms Bailey's former wife she had nothing but praise for the person who had been her husband. She described her as 'totally selfless' and said she would make an excellent Mayor.

Then last week, on Joe Duffy's radio programme, a person in Dublin who is undergoing preparation for a sex change related a rather different experience. She was born a man and for many, many years has been bullied by local thugs because, she thinks, she keeps herself to herself. Her life seems to be entirely dominated by the behaviour of local children. She chooses to do her shopping only in the early morning when the children are at school. Once they get out, she stays in.

She wears feminine tops and trousers but not skirts or dresses. In order to receive sex-change surgery in the UK she will have to live as a woman for a year and then be assessed. But to do that is impossible where she lives. If she left her apartment dressed fully as a woman, she would not, as she put it, know what was waiting for her at the bottom of the stairs. To venture out in women's clothes would require a degree of courage and recklessness that few possess.

At one level, her story is simply about the acceptance of low-grade thuggery at official and community level. Her story also, however, shows that while persons with a sex change in one setting may become the mayor of a city, there are other settings in which such a venture is very risky indeed.

On reading such stories the question will, no doubt, arise in many people's minds as to how successful these sex changes are and whether they bring people the improvements they hope for in their lives. There is now some interesting evidence that indeed surgery to change gender from male to female is largely successful and that those who have such surgery are largely pleased with the results.

The research was done by the University Hospitals of Leicester NHS Trust in the UK. Researchers looked at the early experiences of more than two hundred patients and they did detailed follow-ups with another seventy. In the early stages, almost nine out of ten patients were happy. What was the situation after more time had passed? The research team was only able to conduct detailed interviews with seventy longer term patients. This, they explained, is because people who have this operation want to get on with a new life and therefore can be hard for researchers to contact.

Of the seventy (average age forty-three years), more than three-quarters were happy with their appearance following surgery. Eight out of ten said their general expectations had been met, according to a report on the research in the journal *BJU International*.

So it looks as though sex-change operations work well and that this phenomenon is increasingly accepted by families and, in most cases, by society at large.

All of which throws into question the whole nature of identity and how we define ourselves. But that's another story.

Men, women and violence

John Wayne saunters into a homestead in the Wild West. A woman in there is very mad at him, or perhaps just at strangers in general. She aims a rifle at him and she threatens to shoot unless he gets out and keeps going. But good old John Wayne just walks towards her as she keeps threatening to shoot.

I am sitting in the cinema saying, 'Pull the trigger, please pull the trigger', but it never happens. As always, in a cliché repeated in many Westerns, the woman lacks the mettle to shoot the hero. Instead, the hero gently takes the rifle from her soft, female hands and proceeds to talk sense into her. Women, poor dears, are so nurturing and peaceable by nature that they cannot bring themselves to shoot even John Wayne. Worse, the audience knows that by the time the movie is over, she will want to have his babies.

A woman, it all implies, wouldn't be much use when tough deeds, man-deeds, need doing. Still less would she be much use if you were going out hunting bad guys, as evidenced by that other cinema cliché in which the woman tells the hero 'I'm going along with you whether you like it or not' and ends up having to be rescued by said hero when she gets herself into trouble.

And if women are not able to bring themselves to shoot at guys then they will hardly be able to head sales teams, run corporations or lift heavy weights, even with the help of a forklift truck – gosh those prongs might hurt somebody!

In other words, the image of the non-violent woman suited a society which sought to keep women in the kitchen, the typing pool, the nursery and the hospital ward. Needless to say, the work for which women were considered fit was poorly paid relative to some, though not all, of the work done by men.

The image of the soft, sensitive female, therefore, did not always serve women well. Although that image is gradually changing, it still has a major influence on our thinking and sometimes it does not serve men well either.

The idea of men as violent towards women is easy to accept as true. Rape, whether as an act of personal power or an act of war, provides a non-arguable example.

Yet female suicide bombers walk into cafés and blow men, other women and children apart with premeditation. On the streets of Western cities there is growing concern about the phenomenon of violent female gangs who target other females. And evidence of violent behaviour by women towards their partners is now frequently published. A recent American study examined the subsequent behaviour of people who had been persistently violent as teenagers. The study by the University of Washington found that such people were significantly more likely than others to be violent towards their partners later on. Interestingly, nearly twice as many women as men in the study admitted being violent towards a partner in the previous year.

Here, a 2005 survey by a GP registrar Dr Caitriona Waters found, according to a subsequent report in *The Irish Times*, that 18 per cent of male patients attending a Galway practice had experienced domestic abuse in the past. The same was true of 39 per cent of female patients. She suggested that the figure for men might be an underestimate because men are less likely to attend a GP.

The truth is usually less comfortable than the myths with which we cover over divisions in society. Yet the truth is better because until you know the truth you are not dealing with reality. And the myth, as I mentioned before, also worked to the disadvantage of women by justifying their exclusion from many areas of work.

So in many ways, and paradoxical as it may seem, the growing realisation that females are violent too tears down a myth of inherent gentleness which did not always serve women well – any more than it serves men well now.

Mid-life crisis: the bitter and the sweet

Most men sooner or later hit a point at which they begin to wonder if they've really achieved anything at all in life. They convince themselves that they have wasted their potential and have let themselves down.

This sort of thinking is generally thought to belong to a 'mid-life crisis' but I'm not sure that's accurate. I had my crisis when I was in my mid-twenties and not (I hope) in the middle of my life.

The seventeenth century poet John Milton had his in his early twenties. Somewhere around the time of his twenty-fourth birthday he wrote:

> How soon hath Time, the subtle thief of youth,
> stolen on his wing my three and twentieth year!
> My hasting days fly on with full career,
> but my late spring no bud or blossom shew'th.

Had he lived today he could have felt even more guilty about what he regarded as his lack of achievement. We live in an era in which the pursuit of happiness is not just a right but a duty and in which we are conned into thinking that we should all be able to fulfil our potential.

There are books that will offer to enable you to change your life in anything from seventy days to (I kid you not) ten minutes. There's even a book, the young Milton would no doubt be depressed to learn, called *Ten Poems to Change Your Life*.

I am afraid I am not a supporter of the Be Happy! Achieve Your Potential! movement. Suppose you are working to support your family. Can you at the same time achieve your potential to be an opera singer, an explorer and a best-selling author? Suppose you are caring for a chronically ill relative: can you also achieve your potential to be the Disco King or a Zen monk? No, you cannot.

The late Thérèse Brady, who was a hugely influential figure in Irish psychology, had the following to say in a lecture to the Psychological Society of Ireland in 1990 about the 'human potential movement':

> It legitimised the goal of the good life for all. And yet ... it intensified the misery of those who were unhappy when they contrasted their state with what they perceived to be the state of perpetual joy and fulfilment of the rest of the world.

She was director of post-graduate training in clinical psychology at University College Dublin. She was also one of the architects of the Irish Hospice Foundation and she noted that people can even feel guilty about being bereaved in an age that has, as she put it, 'outlawed distress'.

I wonder how much does the guilt about unfulfilled potential and about the unhappiness that is part of the package deal of life contribute to depression among young men in their twenties? How much does it contribute to the high rate of suicide in this group? And I wonder how much pain is experienced by older men whose dreams have not all come true and who have to accept the reality that some of those dreams will never come true?

It is, of course, a good and healthy thing to try to achieve things you want to achieve. But it is important to be able to recognise that trying to achieve something in one area means you have to drop the expectation of achieving something in another area. If you have worked all the hours God sent you to support a family or to keep a roof over your head then you will not have had time to become a concert pianist and you should resist the temptation to beat yourself up over this fact.

The same goes for the notion of permanent happiness. Such an idea is pure fantasy. If you were happy all the time you simply would not be human.

I am not suggesting pessimism as a way of life. I am suggesting that life is a pretty strong brew and that we need to develop the capacity to taste the bitter as well as the sweet.

A man or a mouse? Er ...

Are you a man or a mouse?

Personally, I tend towards the mouse end of the scale. With a few exceptions, I like to approach confrontation very slowly and preferably from a long way off. In some part of my mind I feel a bit guilty about this. I'd quite like to be the John Wayne character who can take on anybody and anything and who can, with the strength of his personality, let alone his six-shooter, face down the enemy in double-quick time.

Why would I like to be that character? Because I would get my way more often? That's not it. I am quite convinced that having a good relationship with people will get you far more of what you want than throwing your weight around, unless you're in a weight-throwing competition. I think it's because somewhere along the line I got, or was given, the impression that to be a real man you have to be a bit of a John Wayne and if you're not a bit of a John Wayne then you're not a real man.

What are the characteristics of a real man? Well, if you are a real man:

- You talk in a loud, manly voice;
- You can drink a lot and it doesn't affect your judgement;
- You make all the important decisions in the home;
- You never let women boss you around;
- You never let other men boss you around, unless they are also real men;
- You boss your kids around;
- You refuse to go to the doctor when you're sick;

- If anybody wants a fight, you'll fight 'em, by God;
- You never discuss your feelings unless you've been fatally wounded by the Apaches and are about to expire in the dust;
- Your main emotional state is anger, though you'd never use a girlie word such as 'emotional'.

There's a gazillion other characteristics I could list but I still arrive at the sad fact that I am not a real man. Are you a real man? You know, I don't think you are because, to be honest, I don't think real men read articles like this. Worse, this whole book does not contain a single racecard, football result or news item about boxing.

Actually, look around you. How many John Waynes do you see out there? Oh, there are some – but I'll bet they are in a tiny minority. Most of the men out there are not real men at all. They're going to work and trying to get along with their wives and kids or their girlfriends, and they'd rather not get into a fight than get into one. And I bet some of them feel a little twinge of guilt about it all, now and then. They see the guy swaggering around with the baseball cap, the blade-two haircut, the t-shirt and the beerbelly and they suddenly feel inadequate.

If I may digress, where do these guys learn to swagger? Is there some kind of course you can take where they teach you how to do that? Is it the same course where real girls learn to sashay along the street?

It's all a con, isn't it? Real men, as portrayed over many decades by Hollywood, are not representative of their gender at all. Instead they are representative of an idea about men that got passed down to us but that was never actually true. And who knows, maybe some of the real men would like to be able to drop the act, walk normally and let someone else be strong some of the time. After all, even the real man's real man, Tony Soprano, is going to a counsellor.

So perhaps those of us, i.e. the majority, who are not real men should shrug off all this nonsense and assert our right to be as we are without feeling a need to be John Wayne, Tony Soprano or Desperate Dan.

Right, that's it, I'm outta here. Gotta go wrestle a steer to the ground.

The other spouse in the office

How do you think you would like it, Mr New Man, if your missus came home from work singing the praises of her 'office spouse'? How do you think she would react if you came home burbling about how well your office spouse understands you?

The office spouse is a growing phenomenon in the US, the UK and, I suspect, in Ireland too. The phrase refers to a non-sexual but close relationship between two people of opposite genders in the workplace. So well established is the concept that a columnist in the *Financial Times*, which doesn't joke about things like this, announced earlier this year that she was looking for her seventh office spouse. Even Condoleeza Rice is said to have an office spouse. Yep, it's George Bush. The speculation about their relationship began when she referred to George W. as 'my husb ...' at a dinner party.

So what are some characteristics of the office spouse relationship? Basically, it is made up of two people who work together and respect and like each other. They talk to each other about events in their personal lives and not just about business matters. They like each other's company. They go to lunch together. They get coffee for each other. Each shares office gossip with the other before they share it with anybody else. They console each other about the vagaries of their managers and colleagues. They know each other's birthdays and the main events of their family lives. If they fancy each other – and they don't have to – they avoid crossing the line into the bedroom.

Needless to say, their colleagues spot all of this and wonder what, if anything, is going on. They speculate that there might be more to it than an office relationship and they snigger about 'pillow talk'. But this doesn't actually bother the office spouses.

While the phrase 'office spouse' is fairly new, I would imagine that most people who have worked in big organisations have observed such relationships or have had such relationships themselves. The office spouse provides a level of warmth, mutual support, respect and affection that might otherwise be lacking in the workplace.

The big question, though, is whether there is a likelihood that the office spouse relationship will spill over into an affair that could end up wrecking marriages. It seems to me that this kind of relationship is fairly healthy so long as both parties are getting on with their own separate lives outside the office. However, if one of the two is putting their outside relationships on hold in the hope of becoming intimate with the office spouse, then what is going on is damaging. After all, where will you be when the office spouse moves on to a new job?

Keeping the relationship secret, having late dates and dinners, and choosing to spend time outside of work with the office spouse rather than the real spouse are all danger signals. Texting each other outside of work may also be a sign that the relationship is in danger of tipping over into something more serious. And if you are running into the bathroom or out to the car to text the office spouse, it's time to think of ending the relationship.

Having said that, I am not aware of evidence that the office spouse relationship is especially dangerous. I suspect many people have got a lot of valuable emotional support over the years from their office spouses without having done anything at all inappropriate. Human nature being what it is, though, I also have no doubt that some of these relationships have ended in tears.

I am afraid I am not in a position to test out the office spouse phenomenon myself: as a self-employed person, my only colleague at the office is Sheeba, the Scottish Terrier.

But if you've got an office spouse and your real spouse is raising objections, you can always argue that what's good enough for Condoleeza Rice and George Bush is good enough for ... oh, forget it.

Grab a granny

Once upon a time, older women used to go around wearing headscarves and shapeless raincoats as they staggered home with bags of shopping or made their way to the church to say their prayers. Now all that has changed. The traditional older woman has either disappeared or is fast on the way out.

US research shows that your older woman, far from saying her prayers, is working out at the gym and dating younger guys. According to the research, done for the American Association of Retired Persons, just over 30 per cent of unmarried women in their forties, fifties and sixties are in relationships with younger men.

The older women/younger men thing first arrived in the consciousness of some of us in the 1960s when Mrs Robinson sent pulses racing among men in the audiences for *The Graduate*. The most recent cinematic outing for this sort of thing was, I think, the 2003 movie *The Mother*, in which a not terribly glamorous granny has a fling with her daughter's boyfriend. Crikey, it's a long way from daily mass-going isn't it?

This trend is exemplified by celebrities such as Gwyneth Paltrow, Emma Thompson, Madonna, Susan Sarandon and Goldie Hawn: all hitched up with younger men till divorce do them part. But real people do it too. Closer to home, an analysis of marriage statistics over three and a half decades in Britain showed that the proportion of brides marrying men younger than themselves almost doubled to 26 per cent between 1963 and 1998.

Now, we're not talking about cradle-robbers here. In most cases, the man was less than six years younger than the woman. Still, we're seeing a change in society in which the traditional expectation that the man will be at least a year or two older than his bride is fast becoming irrelevant.

No doubt, the trend is also occurring in Ireland, as is the phenomenon of women in their forties and upwards dating younger men. Indeed there is a weekly disco in a Dublin hotel that I have been told is called 'Grab a Granny Night'.

But if glamorous grannies are out boogying the night away with young Adonises (alright, a slight exaggeration but you'd be surprised what enough vodka and coke can do to the perception), where are the older men? I am afraid that one of the problems the older man faces, according to the gloriously named Dr Pepper Schwartz (a sociologist at the University of Washington, and something of an expert on anything and everything to do with sexuality, relationships and all that), is that he lets himself go. By letting himself go, she doesn't mean he puts flowers in his hair and cavorts around a campfire at night chanting 'Om'. She means not paying attention to his appearance, becoming a couch potato, looking like he was dragged through a hedge backwards, that sort of thing. After all that working out and attention to their appearance, she explains, older women are more likely to be attracted to younger men who have kept themselves trim.

Traditionally it used to be said that women let themselves go when they reached a certain age. No more. All has changed utterly. Look at all those tens of thousands of women running or walking in the women's mini-marathon. That's what we're up against, lads, as we cling to our cans of lager and sink deeper into the couch.

Any older man hoping to attract one of these older women for himself will have to go to work: get down to the gym, start pounding the pavements in his jogging gear, replace his pint with a still water and his fry with a bowl of muesli – and maybe get himself down to Colour Me Beautiful to get his dress sense sorted out.

By the way, if you're a younger woman you needn't be smirking at us guys. If you happen to have a boyfriend about whom you're crazy and if you're the jealous type, just remember it's not your girlfriends you need to worry about. It's their mothers.

The women are coming!

I don't know why, but I have always tended to think of dentists as male. The idea of a woman seeking your views on world politics while filling your mouth with hideous instruments as you gurgle pathetically has never seemed quite right.

Last year more women than men signed up for courses in dentistry, so before long it will be a woman who will be wielding the drill. It is all part of the female future. If present trends continue we will have more female doctors, lawyers, vets and dentists as new graduates enter the workforce and old chaps retire.

And it is not only in Ireland that this is happening. Under the recent headline 'Swedish women to overtake stupid men', an article in English-language Swedish newspaper *The Local*, reported similar trends: 'There will soon be a large collective of uneducated, low-paid men who don't have any friends, and are unmarried and alone – as well as uninteresting for women looking for a relationship' the newspaper reported researcher Ingemar Gens (a man) as saying.

We are also getting fatter than women and we are less intelligent than them, according to Gens. Soon the only remaining men-only area will be the Catholic episcopacy. Not a very jolly picture is it? Here are all these women running the show, taking all the good jobs that we kept them out of for decades and decades, while we sit around getting fat and waiting for some woman to make an honest man of us.

Will they, do you think, still make the dinner and do the housework when they come home in their top-of-the-range phallic-symbol cars from their spacious offices? Or will they expect us to get off our backsides and throw a pizza in the oven?

But there are upsides to this. For instance, women have babies. It's only in the last couple of decades that industries and organisations run by men have become friendly towards this fact. Can we expect organisations run by women to take a more human approach? Can we expect them to embrace the needs of workers, male and female, to spend time caring for their families and to work flexibly if necessary to achieve this?

Let's hope so. However, it seems to me that women who do not have children can get quite impatient with the child-tending needs of colleagues who are working mothers, so perhaps things might not change as much as you would think, which is a pity. Nevertheless, the ascendancy of women should lead to some marginal improvements in attitudes towards family issues in the workplace.

And, of course, while the Big Woman is off running the world, we chaps, as soon as the housekeeper has arrived and we have put him to work, can climb into the SUV and pop down to the gym to sweat off some ounces with the female personal trainer. Later we can meet the lads for coffee and a chat in the shopping centre before we head off to collect Tristan from the Montessori.

And when herself comes home exhausted from her battles in the corporate war zone, we could have a nice gin and tonic ready for her and *The Irish Times* open at the Simplex page on which we will not have filled in any of the answers. And then we will go and make the dinner, leaving her in peace to relax after her long day's work. Tristan will be kept in his room until she is ready for some quality time with him.

In other words, we will do all the things for them that they now do for us. If you do not like this scenario and if you want to keep running the world, there is an alternative. According to Gens in an interview with the NVL Dialogweb website (www.nordvux.net), the only exception to the rule that women will take over will be in the Islamic countries.

So if you don't want to go with the flow here in the West perhaps you should begin to make the necessary arrangements.

Men, the true romantics

I sent off for a book once that was supposed to contain the secrets of happiness. Needless to say it didn't work.

It did, however, have one thing to say which you don't often hear and which still strikes me as true. This was that men are the romantics in life and women are the hard-headed pragmatists. We are usually told the opposite: the man in the old ad scaled the walls in his turtleneck pullover to bring a box of Milk Tray to the lady not because he was romantic but because *she* was. And a whole industry is based on the notion that women must have flowers bought for them because they are romantic. But is that really the case?

Is the true romantic not the one who actually buys the flowers and the chocolates and who books the candlelit dinner? The romantic idea of arranging the horse and carriage to bring the daughter to her First Communion is usually, I have little doubt, the man's – and an idea, by the way, which he would do better not to have in the first place.

And you know those little remote-controlled racing cars? I was out in UCD one Saturday afternoon during one otherwise long-forgotten summer when I came across an actual rally consisting of men racing these little cars. They were dressed up in all the gear and some of them even had blonde girlfriends also dressed up in all the gear. The two female arch-feminists I was with on the day howled with laughter, absolutely delighted by this demonstration of the silliness of men.

Let me say at once that it did, actually, look a bit silly, but that's not the point. The point is that only men could romanticise this activity to the extent of dressing up like Michael Schumacher and

PADRAIG O'MORAIN

going off to hold races at Belfield with their toy cars. The arch-feminists, meanwhile, were going off to correct students' assignments – not romantic at all.

But aren't women more intuitive than men and isn't that tied up with the whole romantic-type thing? Er, sorry but that's not true either. Women may think they are more intuitive and may have convinced everybody else that there is a thing called 'feminine intuition', but the evidence suggests otherwise. A recent study of more than 15,000 people for the Edinburgh International Science Festival found that 78 per cent of women and 58 per cent of men considered themselves to be highly intuitive.

Psychologist Richard Wiseman showed them photographs of people smiling. Some had faked their smiles and some were smiling genuinely. It turned out that men were better than women at spotting fake smiles in the opposite sex. Two-thirds – 67 per cent – of women guessed correctly when men were faking their smiles. However, 76 per cent of men could tell that women were faking it. So who's more intuitive?

If it's the case that women have been fooling us into believing they are more romantic than we are, then a few things will have to change. For instance, Mother's Day currently means flowers, chocolates and dinner for the women but Father's Day means three new pairs of socks for the men. It ought to be the other way around.

Not everything has to change, though. Have you seen that billboard promoting the floristry industry which says something like, 'Moody Cow. Don't know what you did wrong? Send her flowers anyway'? It's a brilliant ad that feeds into this idea that there's something more mysterious and romantic about women than there is about us men. So if she's being a moody cow she's not just being a moody cow: she's being something complex that a mere man could not possibly understand, because she's the romantic, intuitive one and he is not.

Guess what, guys? Chances are, she's just being a moody cow, end of mystery. But send her the flowers anyway. Because you, after all, are the romantic and that's the sort of thing romantics do.

Shouldn't non-smokers have smoke breaks too?

Every now and then I spot him: the Greater Crested Executive with his paunch and his pink shirt and his tie and his barrel chest.

He is walking up and down outside his office taking in the air and looking up at the blue sky. He appears to be a man who had a lot on his mind back at his desk – but out here the mental if not the physical weight has lifted. He has that 'this is my moment of freedom' look on his face.

He is out for a cigarette break, of course. It is a pity that his moment of freedom involves engaging in a life-threatening activity. What is even more of a pity is my suspicion that if he ever gives up the cigarettes he will also give up the moments of freedom that punctuate the working day. Instead he will remain chained to the desk and the phone and his laptop just as his non-smoking colleagues are right now.

After all, have you ever seen non-smokers popping out of the office to take the air three or four times a day? It is an odd thing that Mr Mighty, your boss, will graciously accept that you need to 'slip out for a fag' several times during your working day, but if you asked to go out for 'a breath of fresh air' he would be puzzled and quite possibly upset.

What the smokers have discovered, thanks to Micheál Martin (to whom I am sure they are grateful) is that there can be such a thing in the working day as a time when you can be yourself again. During that time you can get away from being wired up to an array of electronic gadgets. You can get your head out of the dramas and worries of office life and you can look at the clouds and the sky and the trees.

These breaks are of the most enormous value for your mental health. They keep your stress levels low and your head clear. It's pretty obvious stuff isn't it? And yet unless we are under the thumb of an addiction that needs to be satisfied we are likely to deny ourselves what might be called these stress breaks because we have too much to do.

Of course, if we were smokers we would not have 'too much to do' because we would see to it that we made the time to go out to get our fix. What that means is that we do actually have time to take breaks during the day, whatever we say to the contrary.

You could always just sit at your desk resenting that chap marching up and down there in his pink shirt smoking a cigarette and smelling the roses. Not that he can actually smell them, but you know what I mean. As he de-stresses, you could increase your blood pressure by muttering to yourself about the extra work you have to do because he is not actually in here doing his work. This is all nonsense because his smoking breaks probably do not actually bring any extra work your way at all. How much better it would be if you went down and joined him, though at a safe distance so that you would not have to breathe in his smoke. Then you could both return to your desks in a relaxed state and you yourself could enjoy a little smug superiority as the one who had not damaged his health during the previous ten minutes.

The same, I suggest, should apply to the pub scene. Why shouldn't non-smokers be entitled to go out to the pub door and chat up strange women just as smokers can?

But what are these breaks to be called? To introduce a new type of break – such as 'health breaks' – could trigger years of industrial relations negotiations. I suggest you take the line of least resistance. Just announce that you're 'off for a smoke break' and nobody will bat an eyelid.

Inappropriate snogging?
Blame it on the emotional
brain!

You know that awful 'Noooooooooooh!' that can galvanise you as you emerge from the depths of sleep and hangover to remember snogging the face off that colleague whom you never really liked and never want to see again for the rest of your life?

Here you are, the morning after the Christmas party and little by little the awful flashbacks parade before you. Surely you did not engage in an ENT session with her in front of the entire office? And what's this? Did your worst enemy really stand there filming the whole thing on his mobile phone?

Oh yes, it's all true. When you return to work you and your colleague will pass each other by in total silence for months, if you're lucky. The buds will be budding and the lambs gambolling in the fields before you speak again. If you are not lucky your colleague will have taken your passion for real and will want you to leave your wife, your children, your trade-up detached house and your SUV and move into her one-bedroom apartment to have babies. If you are really, really unlucky she will ring your wife and ask for a divorce on your behalf.

What is going on here demonstrates the way your brain works – and not just the male brain. Last night, when you were in the throes of public passion, the primitive part of your brain located in your brain stem was in charge. Your primitive brain likes pleasure and hates pain – but it doesn't really bother to figure out the consequences down the road. When comedian Lenny Bruce said 'Men are like dogs' he was talking about the primitive brain. Bruce said that a man being rushed to hospital in an ambulance can still register that the nurse has a nice bottom. That's the primitive brain for you.

So last night your primitive brain and Snogperson's primitive brain were seeking pleasure and didn't care what anybody thought or what the future might hold. What happened to that other part of your brain whose job it is to keep you safe? Unfortunately, it was pickled in alcohol and didn't know it existed.

We could call this the emotional brain. One of its key jobs is to ensure that if you are in danger you get out of there fast, you fight your corner or you freeze until the danger passes you by. Had it been functional, it would have told you last night to stay away from Snogperson and if hers had been functional it would have told her to stay away from you. It would have been instantly aware of the dangers of a frenzied snogging session that, for all you know, is going to end up on youtube.com when your enemy transfers the video from his mobile phone. That's the part of your brain that is screeching at you this morning.

So now you have to figure out what to do. Beg Snogperson to forget about last night? Confess all to your wife? Say nothing and hope for the best? When you start thinking like this, a third part of your brain has entered the fray. This is the logical part that helps you to figure out solutions and possibilities. Needless to say, this part also was out of its tree last night.

So while your emotional brain is having hysterics and your brainstem is gagging for a coffee and a fry, the logical part of your brain is trying to figure a way out of this mess.

What's the solution? I don't know, ask your logical brain. But maybe you'd better cut out this article in case your wife finds out about Snogperson. If you ask her to read it, perhaps she'll understand. Yeah.

Meanwhile, why not move some personal effects – a hot water bottle, a torch – into the doghouse. With luck and a lot of contrition – this is the logical part of your brain speaking now, so listen up – you just might be let out for Christmas Day.

'Tis the season for testosterone

We have entered the season when the chatting up of women by men and men by women reaches manic proportions. Though it may all seem like madness, be assured that old Mother Nature is working away craftily in the background.

Testosterone is the hormone that makes lads lads: boost the level of testosterone in the bloodstream and we start sniffing around for a mate, if only for the night. Lower the testosterone level and we are more likely to behave ourselves.

Mother Nature, the theory of evolution tells us, is primarily interested in ensuring that we pass on our genes and so perpetuate the species. In other words, Mother Nature is interested in promoting the mating game. Chaps who are footloose and fancy free and who want to stay that way are, of course, favourite targets of hers.

For instance, a piece of research conducted at Harvard University found that testosterone levels are higher in single than in married men. They found this out by measuring testosterone in the saliva of men who were married, single or married with children. The single men maintained the highest testosterone levels throughout the day. The lowest were in men who were married with children.

Hence, the single men have testosterone levels that send them off in search of mates, while the married men with children are more likely to stay at home. The researchers suggest that being with their wives and children causes the testosterone of married men to fall. One wonders if this explains the adulterous activities of some of those Jack the Lads who spend as little time as possible with their families?

When our testosteroned male goes off looking for a mate, sly old Mother Nature is at hand again. A team at the University of Chicago paid male students to have their saliva tested at a laboratory. A young, female research assistant 'happened' to be in the lab. Naturally, the male students chatted to her. When their saliva was tested it transpired that chatting to her had boosted their levels of testosterone by up to one-third. The men with the highest testosterone increase were the ones who later said they found her particularly attractive. And here is the scary bit, guys: before she had seen the test results, the lab assistant was able to say, accurately, who these men were.

Transpose that experiment to the heated and intoxicated atmosphere of an office Christmas party and the results hardly bear thinking about.

Other research at the Institute of Applied Psychology in Lisbon found that men who were trying for a baby with their partner had higher testosterone levels. Their levels of testosterone appeared to peak during periods of intense sexual activity. Some experts believe that in these cases the man is responding to his partner's pheromones (chemical messengers) – without realising it, he is synchronising his testosterone level to that point in her cycle when she has the greatest chance of conceiving.

Pheromones, by the way, are also thought to explain why women who live together tend to have their periods around the same time.

With all these chemicals flying around, how come people are not attracted, generally speaking, to blood relatives? According to British psychologist Dr John Marsden, the answer lies in our sense of smell. It appears that variations in our immune systems change the way we smell to other people. Blood relatives with similar immune systems to our own smell differently to strangers with immune systems unlike ours – the difference helps to switch off the attraction to relatives.

By all these strategies old Mother Nature, who is by no means the butter-wouldn't-melt-in-her-mouth figure she is often made out to be, keeps us breeding and mixing genes. So much for free will! When you get hitched up to your partner for life it has more to do with chemistry than you might imagine.

And when your partner tells you in the course of a blazing row that, 'I don't know what I saw in you' you can reply: 'You're right. You don't.'

Life begins at, er ...

A fan website for the TV series *One Foot in the Grave* says of the series: 'it brings home the realisation that Victor and Margaret are what we have to look forward to.'

Actually, the research suggests, it does not have to be like that at all. In the series, Victor Meldrew is the very cross, very grumpy, very angry old man. Margaret is his long-suffering wife. However, as you age, you are probably less likely rather than more likely to turn into a grumpy old man or woman. Contrary to common impressions, the older we get the more likely we are to focus on positive rather than negative things.

In a piece of research published in the journal *Psychology and Ageing*, young and old people were shown photographs of faces depicting positive or negative emotions. When their eye movements were tracked, it turned out that the young people spent longer looking at those faces that depicted fear. The older people spent most time looking at the pictures of happy faces. The researchers concluded that older people focus more on the positive in order to maintain their emotional well-being.

It is not just a matter of emotional well-being. Optimism appears to boost physical well-being as well – or at least to be closely associated with it. Dutch researchers tracked the health of 999 men and women aged 65 to 85 for 9 years. (Just what the attraction of the number nine was for the researchers I do not know – maybe it's a Dutch thing.) What they found was that those participants who, at the start, described themselves as highly optimistic had a 55 per cent lower general risk of death. Their risk of death from heart failure was 23 per cent lower than that of the more gloomy fellows. Both men and women benefited equally from optimism in relation to heart attacks.

Why should this be so? Is somebody up there doling out rewards to optimists and punishments to pessimists? Well, no, the answer is more mundane than that and has nothing to do with the supernatural. The researchers pointed out that people who are pessimistic may be more likely to smoke, eat too much, over-indulge in alcohol and engage in other habits that are bad for their health. They may also be more likely to suffer hypertension.

Of course, health in old people tends to be less good than health in young people. But that fact does not necessarily condemn old people to a state of gloom. Researchers in California spoke to 500 Americans aged 60 to 98, all of whom had had health problems of various kinds. The researchers asked them how well they believed themselves to be ageing, on a scale of 1 to 10, with 10 being the best. On average, they gave themselves a score of 8.4. That's probably a fairly good score at any age, let alone when you've had to fight off cancer, heart disease and other threats.

What the findings seem to suggest is that how good you feel about yourself mentally and emotionally is affected by factors other than your physical health. In other words, people who are gloomy in old age because of their physical disabilities may actually be gloomy people anyhow.

Of course, this is all terribly easy for me to sit here and say – but if I live long enough to test out all this research, I will be sure to let you know how it worked out.

However, it seems safe to assume that if you are an optimistic sort of person you have something to be pleased about: there is a good chance that your optimism will continue and will protect your well-being for life. Then again, if you are an optimistic person you probably believe that already.

If you're a pessimist, I hope that even you might agree that these findings provide a powerful incentive for walking on the bright side of the street.

So cheer up. Accentuate the positive. Don't become a Victor Meldrew.

Clock time and lived time

More fathers than mothers, I expect, are in danger of discovering some day that their children have grown up while they were busy at work.

Increasingly, there are women who feel they face the same danger. But the point normally arrives when the woman decides to remain in the home more or less full-time until the children have at least finished primary school. (The Labour Force Survey by the Central Statistics Office shows that in 2007, a total of 523,000 women were on 'home duties' compared to 6,000 men.)

Sometimes, however, the couple cannot make that choice. Huge mortgages have done a lot to narrow parents' choices. For the man who is the main earner, it is all too easy to get caught up in the world of work to an extent that leaves no time for children, partner or, even, himself.

Maybe it's time to do something about that. The US and Canada are currently in the middle of a 'Take Back Your Time' month. The campaign (www.timeday.org) urges people at work to 'reclaim' at least four periods of time during the month. This is time they will spend with family or engaged in activities for themselves alone – but which takes them out of the workplace.

A key idea behind the campaign is that we make a great effort to maximise what we can get done from nine to five – but we should pay much more attention to what we do between five and nine. That, after all, is the time when involvement with children or other family is most likely to be possible. Yet some of us have a habit of getting our second wind around seven in the evening and spending that important time at work, performing tasks that could wait until the next day.

These thoughts were prompted, not so much by the North American campaign, as by a book by a Swedish physicist, Bodil Jönsson, called *Ten Thoughts about Time: How to Make More of the Time in your Life*. This is not a time-management manual, packed with tips on how to get more out of your day. Such manuals don't always work anyway. A colleague of mine once used a time-management manual, acquired on an expensive course, to prop up his desk, so at least he felt it had not been a complete waste of money.

Jönsson's very readable book is a philosophical reflection on the role that time plays in our lives. She highlights the difference between 'clock-time' and 'lived-time'. Clock-time refers to all that time during which we have one eye on the clock because we're rushing to the next meeting or trying to get a certain number of things done in the day. Lived-time, by contrast, refers to periods when you can be yourself, when you are not trying to meet a deadline, when you are not trying to pack two hours' work into sixty minutes. Lived-time could be spent having a meal with friends, playing with the kids, going for a walk, reading a novel or talking to your partner.

Jönsson suggests that we need more lived-time, and few of us would disagree. She notices how lived-time is disappearing even out of the lives of children. Many of us can remember long, eternal summers during school holidays. What we are remembering is an experience of lived-time. Today's schoolchildren are so busy rushing from the summer project to the tennis camp to the music camp that they are living in clock-time all summer.

Jönsson encourages us to reflect on the difference between these two kinds of time, on the value of lived-time and on the need to make more room for it. How are you to do this, you may ask? I don't have a trick to help you to do it and neither does she, but if you make an effort to realise the tyranny that clock-time exercises over you, I think you will come up with ways that suit your needs.

This book was a massive bestseller when it was first published in Sweden. Its message is just as relevant for the children of the Celtic Tiger and for the men, women and children on whose time the Tiger feeds.

The walking cure

I don't suppose you'd be impressed if you went to your GP because you felt a bit down in yourself and you were told to go take a walk in the park.

However, research published in the UK last week suggests that a walk in the park may be just what we all need. The mental health organisation, Mind, decided to examine the mental health benefits of what it called 'green' exercise. The results were quite astonishing.

I should point out that 'green' exercise has nothing to do with members of the Green Party trudging from door to door seeking your vote. Rather it refers to taking a walk in a country park, gardening and such activities.

A total of 108 people involved in green exercise activities with local Mind groups were surveyed. A remarkable proportion, 94 per cent, said their mental health had benefited. They reported feeling better about themselves and having a sense of achievement, having greater self-esteem and greater motivation.

The key thing is that not only was some sort of physical exercise involved but that it involved contact with nature. It has been known for quite some time that exercise lifts your mood. What this latest study tells us is that the big benefits come from exercise in a 'green' setting. For example, 90 per cent of people who took an outdoor walk in a country park reported a boost in their self-esteem. Of those who took an indoor walk in a shopping centre, 44 per cent actually reported a reduction. So much for retail therapy!

Of those who were depressed 71 per cent reported an improvement in their mood from an outdoor walk compared to 45 per cent from a walk around the shopping centre. Indeed, 22 per cent reported that a walk around a shopping centre made their depression worse – I bet they were the guys. Of people suffering from tension, 71 per cent felt better after a walk in the park compared to 28 per cent of those who walked around a shopping centre. And – no surprise here – 50 per cent of those who walked around the shopping centre felt even more stressed at the end.

The benefits of ecotherapy, as it is called, are taken more seriously on the Continent than here. Hundreds of therapeutic farms exist to which people go to do farm work to boost their mental health.

There is a historical significance to this. Those big old psychiatric hospitals, which are gradually being replaced with wards in general hospitals, all had farms attached. The farms provided many of the food needs of these institutions but they were also seen, when the hospitals were built, as conducive to the mental health of patients.

As the Mind report put it: 'The principles behind ecotherapy are not new. In the past, mental health institutions were often situated in pleasant gardens and natural landscapes. But these considerations no longer play a significant role in the planning of urban and rural space in the design of hospitals, the treatment and care of people experiencing mental distress or the identification of public health and social care priorities.'

In the light of that, look at the total disregard that planners and developers have shown for the provision of pleasant green spaces in the design of housing estates and apartment complexes over many years. Look at the ugliness of the setting of health centres and indeed of many modern hospitals. Is it any wonder that we have seen increases in depression? It's as if we are cut off from our very souls.

The message for mental health services is this: enabling people with mental health problems to take part in activities in a pleasant, green environment is far preferable to relying on medication alone.

And the message for the rest of us? If you want to feel better, get off the sofa and get back to nature.

Hearing voices – more
common than we think

Ever thought your mobile phone was ringing when it wasn't? In that fairly common experience the sound, or the sensation in the case of a vibrating phone, is produced by your own brain. Or perhaps you thought somebody was calling your name when in fact nobody was doing so. Again, a not uncommon experience that we shrug off as a mistake.

Now move to the other end of the spectrum: hearing voices that condemn or praise you or order you around, voices that feel absolutely real but which are produced by your own brain. This can be a pretty upsetting experience if people take these voices seriously or if they assume that hearing voices means they are mentally ill.

It is true to say that a significant proportion of people with schizophrenia hear voices. Does that mean that a significant proportion of people who hear voices have schizophrenia? Dutch research back in the 1980s would suggest that more people than we might imagine live normal, well-functioning lives despite their voices.

Dr Marius Romme, the psychiatrist who conducted the research, suggested that those who lived normal lives were people who accepted their voices, who knew the voices had no control over them and who had developed coping techniques. He believed that struggling with the voices and trying to suppress them just made them stronger and greatly distressed the person suffering from them.

It appears that the voices people hear in their heads are usually male. Some researchers suggest this is because the female voice is more complex. So if your brain is going to produce a fake voice, it takes the easy option and goes for the male version. Sorry guys. Some people hear voices that are harsh and condemning. Others are more fortunate: the voices are affectionate and caring. There are some reasons to believe that persons who were abused as children may be more likely than others to hear voices and that these often sound like the voices of their abusers.

The key thing about the voices is that they are indeed a fake. It is when the person imagines that the voices are real that the experience is more likely to be harmful. So if you hear voices it is vital to understand that they are not real and that they have no control over you, whatever they may say.

Indeed, rather than running away from the voices, some people advocate observing them in a detached sort of way, distinguishing between good and bad voices, perhaps talking back to them to try to work out what they mean but always in the knowledge that they are fake.

Talking to other people who hear voices or talking to a counsellor is also helpful – though at the very beginning the voices may become more intense for a while. The Mental Health Foundation in the UK suggests that people who have been prescribed medication for hearing voices find it helpful to ask other 'voice hearers' what medications work for them.

The key point is that if you hear voices you need not go around feeling like an outcast. Unknown to you, people you meet every day may have the same experience. If hearing voices is having a serious effect on your life then you may need to join a self-help group, talk to a doctor or seek counselling.

Should you talk about it to work colleagues? Personally, I would not. There is so much ignorance and prejudice about the subject that to do so would be unwise.

The Dutch research by Dr Romme led to the establishment of self-help groups. One such group is the Hearing Voices Network, which was founded in Manchester in 1988. Its website is www.hearing-voices.org.

If you hear voices, I suggest you also look at www.mentalhealth.org.uk, the website of the Mental Health Foundation. Click on 'Mental Health A–Z' and follow the alphabetical list to find a helpful page on the subject.